FRISKY PHONICS FUN 1

Written and illustrated
by Barbara Bachman

Cover design by Barbara Bachman
Cover by Tom Sjoerdsma
Copyright © Good Apple, Inc., 1984
Printing No. 987654
ISBN No. 0-86653-195-5

GOOD APPLE, INC.
BOX 299
CARTHAGE, IL 62321-0299

TABLE OF CONTENTS

LETTER TO THE TEACHER

Dear Teacher:

If you are looking for a comprehensive phonics workbook that can capture and "keep" student interest, then *Frisky Phonics Fun* is for you! Through a host of reproducible and beautifully illustrated discussion pages, activities, games, and performance work sheets, you will cultivate the application of phonics in a way that will stir up a child's enthusiasm! Five friendly little cartoon mutts will entertain your entire classroom as they help you to ensure the sufficient student mastery of basic word-attack skills.

Book One is a structured study of **one-syllable words having short vowel sounds.** Students can begin working with Book One *after* they have mastered single-consonant sounds. Book One will expose the beginning reader to over 1,000 words!

Using the Dogtown dogs as your classroom motivators, you will introduce, review and reinforce:

1. single-consonant and vowel recognition
2. short vowel sounds
3. initial consonant blends
4. final consonant blends
5. consonant digraphs

Frisky Phonics Fun will provide refreshing new ways to strengthen *both* spelling and reading comprehension skills. Activities will involve:

1. discussing and identifying letters and their sounds
2. reading and spelling words from structured word lists
3. substituting consonants to build and spell rhyming words
4. writing words to name pictures on gameboards
5. reading and answering questions and riddles
6. associating pictures with descriptive sentences
7. substituting vowels to build new words
8. playing lots of unique spelling/reading games to practice, apply and master basic word patterns.

The sight words most frequently used throughout Book One are:

or	you	I	put	a	see	to	name
for	your	he	do	the	find	into	have
so	her	she					

As we bring laughter and excitement to your creative teaching endeavors, we wish you happiness with *Frisky Phonics Fun*.

Barbara Bachman
and
The Friendly Folks at Good Apple, Inc.

Vowels

5 very special letters in the alphabet

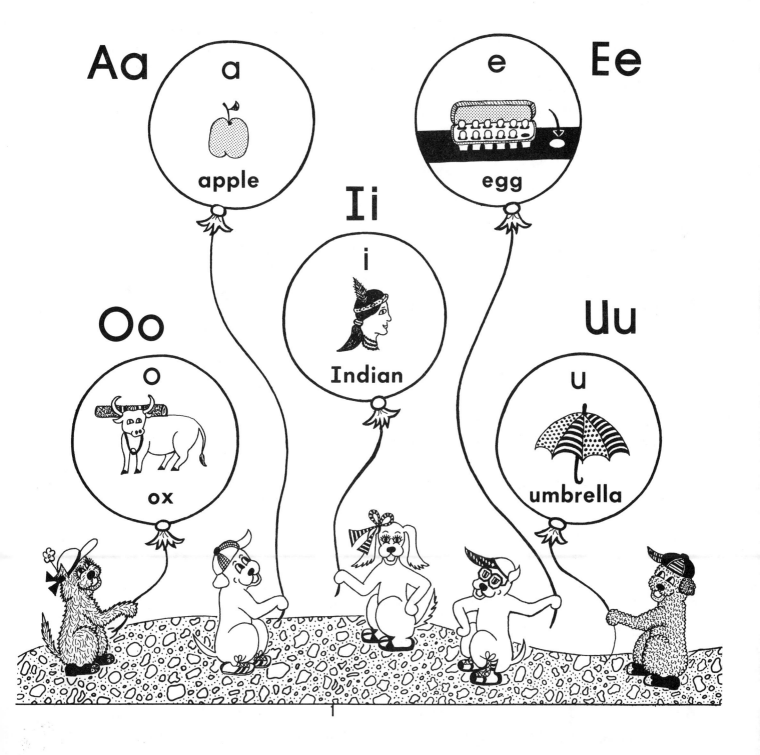

Aa · a · apple

e · egg · Ee

Ii · i · Indian

Oo · o · ox

Uu · u · umbrella

VOWELS
5 Very Important Letters

abcdefghijklmnopqrstuvwxyz = 26

There are 26 letters in the alphabet.

5 of these letters are called vowels → a e i o u.

 Circle all of the vowels in the box below.

k d w g u t n f e c o h s i m v b

a c m u z l o j u d x p a f w e k

h b e s i v u k a n g y t q o r d

f k l a t e p u x i z d a u q m o

b u g d s t o w j e y n v b a c i

e h a w l u i p e t k a q r o u g

2

Consonants

21 special letters
in the alphabet

If a letter is **not** a vowel, it is a **consonant.**

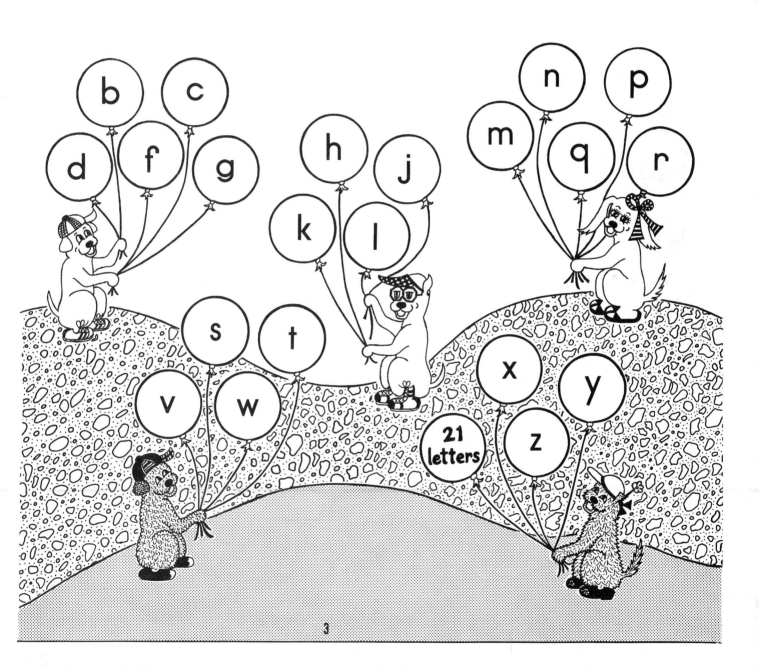

Catch a Consonant

Many letters in our alphabet are called <u>consonants</u>.
A, E, I, O, and U are the vowels.
If a letter is <u>not</u> a vowel, <u>it</u> <u>is</u> <u>a</u> <u>consonant</u>.

Help the dogs catch a consonant!
Color every fish that holds a <u>consonant</u> letter.

b	y	u	g	e	s
o	k	r	c	i	x
h	w	a	q	f	p
v	e	m	u	d	z
j	i	n	t	l	a

DO YOU KNOW YOUR VOWELS AND CONSONANTS?

WELCOME to the

V-C SIDEWALK ROLLER RACE !

The dogs want you to meet them at the DOGTOWN ROLLER RINK for a skating party. To get there, you must <u>race</u> down V-C Sidewalk on roller skates!

YOU WILL NEED :   a skating partner (2 racers)
2 game markers
a gameboard (on page 6)
game cards (on page 7)

Read the directions carefully !

1. Look at the gameboard. Place your game markers on the "<u>START</u>" space.

2. Cut out the <u>game cards</u> on page 7. Each card has a letter on it. Put the letter cards in a pile, face down, on the gameboard.

3. <u>YOU ARE READY TO RACE!</u> Take turns drawing a card. If you draw a <u>consonant</u> letter, skate <u>forward</u> <u>two</u> (2) sidewalk spaces. If you draw a <u>vowel</u>, skate <u>backwards</u> to the <u>nearest</u> doghouse!

4. The first skater to reach the DOGTOWN ROLLER RINK – WINS THE RACE!

MIX UP THE GAME CARDS AND RACE AGAIN !

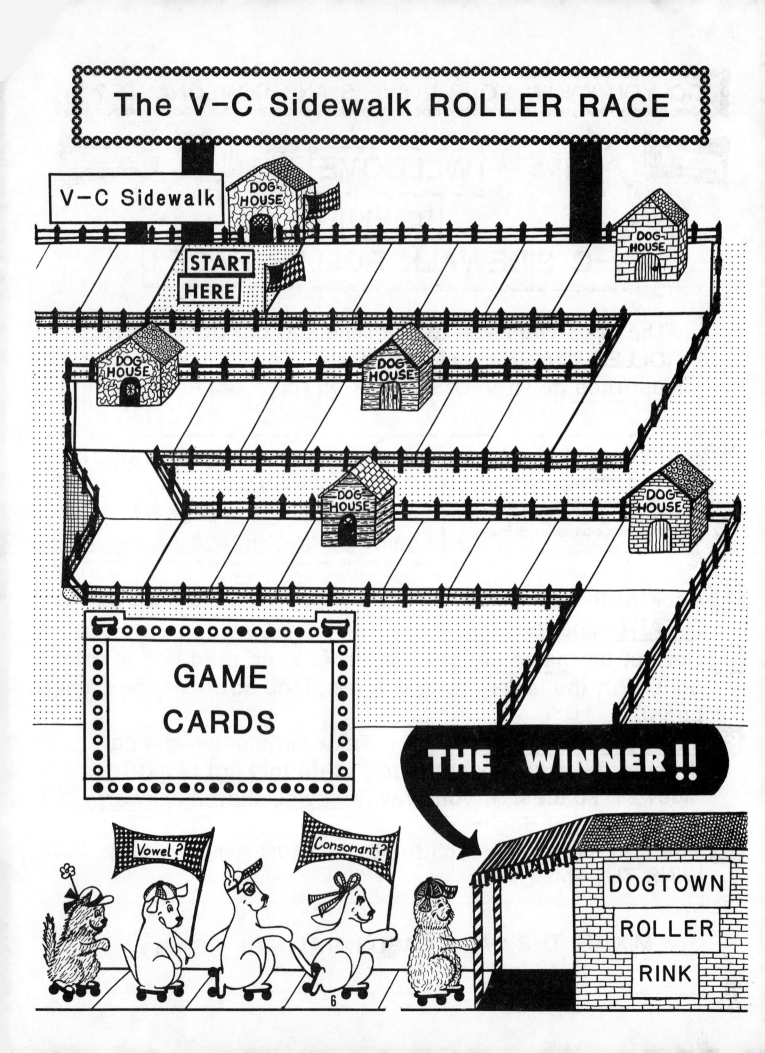

The V-C Sidewalk ROLLER RACE

GAME CARDS

b	k	h	f	d
w	e	c	i	m
a	n	s	v	o
g	u	p	a	z
i	q	e	t	r
y	o	x	l	u
j	b	r	e	c
k	a	d	o	s

7

LET'S TALK ABOUT
the Sound of Short A /a/

apple

ax

TRICK OR TREAT

B.E. BACHMAN
3808 TELLWAY
BOULDER, CO.
80303

8

Words to Read and Spell

an	ad	bag	cap
ban	bad	lag	lap
can	dad	rag	map
fan	fad	nag	nap
man	had	sag	sap
ran	lad	tag	tap
tan	mad	wag	yap
van	sad	gag	gap
pan	pad		

as	ax	at	mat
has	lax	bat	rat
gas	tax	cat	sat
	sax	fat	vat
	wax	hat	pat

ă

gal	
pal	

am	cab
dam	dab
ham	lab
ram	nab
tam	tab
jam	gab
yam	jab

NAMES		
Al	Max	Sam
Dan	Nan	Val
Hal	Pam	Pat

A DOGGONE EXCEPTION
was

Rhyming ă Ladders

Short ă words

NAME _____

DATE _____

 Climb the ladder steps and write the word that names each picture. Read your rhyming words!

_at words

cat

_an words

_ag words

_am words

10

¡CATCH ∗≋∗ THAT ∗≋∗ CAT!¡

THAT CAT SNATCHED OUR BAG OF BONES! HE RAN DOWN SHORT A AVENUE!

Help the dogs catch that cat!
You must run fast down SHORT A AVENUE!
Write the word that names each picture along the way.

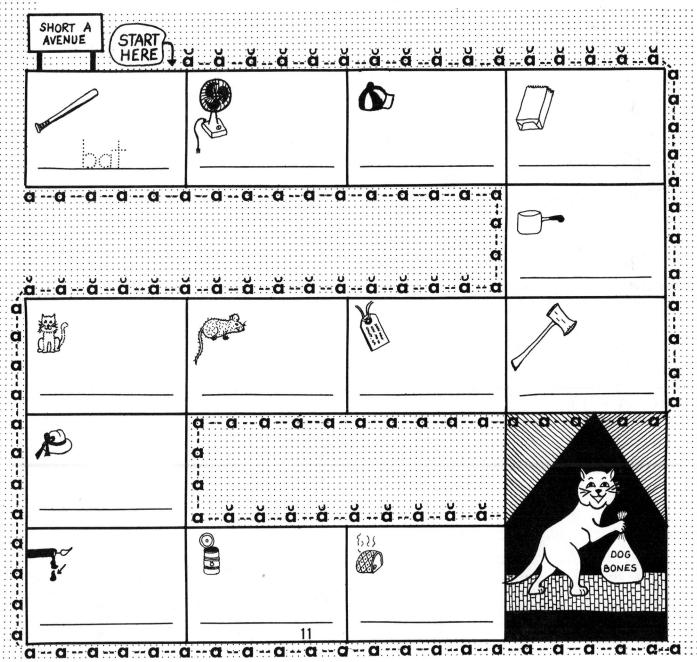

SHORT A AVENUE

START HERE

bat

DOG BONES

11

A SATURDAY AFTERNOON

NAME_____

It's a Saturday afternoon! What can _you_ find at the park?

🐾 Check ⊘ YES or NO.

	YES	NO
Can you find a **bat**?	◯	◯
Can you find a **cap**?	◯	◯
Can you find a **man**?	◯	◯
Can you find a **rat**?	◯	◯
Can you find a **ham**?	◯	◯
Can you find a **pan**?	◯	◯

	YES	NO
Can you find a **cat**?	◯	◯
Can you find a **bag**?	◯	◯
Can you find a **fan**?	◯	◯
Can you find a **hat**?	◯	◯
Can you find a **can**?	◯	◯

12

 Color the things you found!

What's Happening?

NAME _____

DATE _____

There is a sentence under each picture below. The sentence tells us what is happening in the picture. But one word in each sentence is missing. Fill in the blanks and write the missing <u>short ă words</u>.

The man has an _____.

The fat _____ sat.

The rat sat on a _____.

The _____ is mad!

A _____ is on the bag.

CAR * WAX

The _____ is in a can.

Sam has a _____.

A _____ is on his lap.

LET'S TALK ABOUT
the Sound of Short E /e/

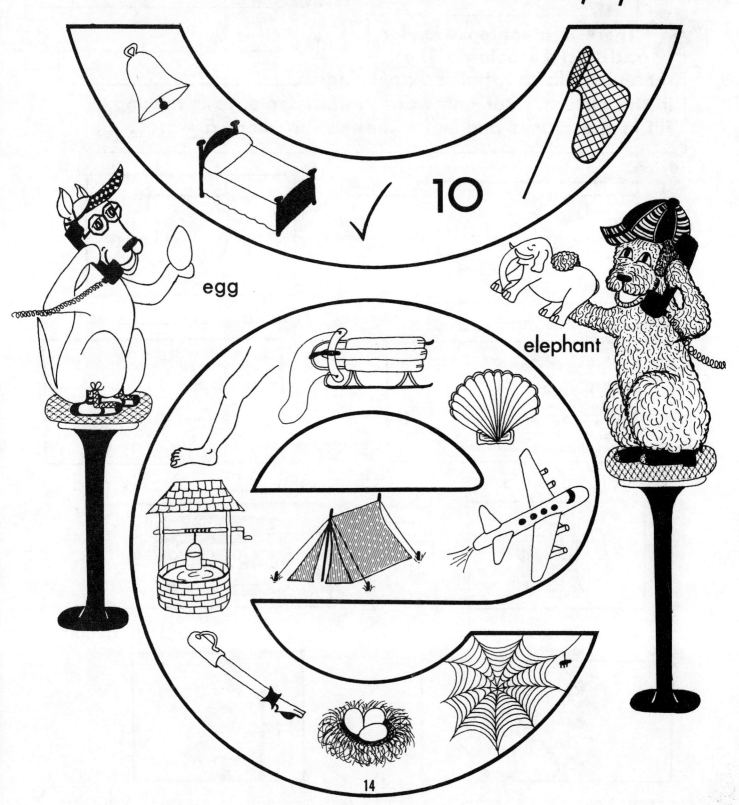

egg

elephant

14

Words to Read and Spell

bet get jet let met net	bed fed led ped wed	den hen men pen ten yen
pet set vet wet yet	beg keg leg peg	hem pep web yes

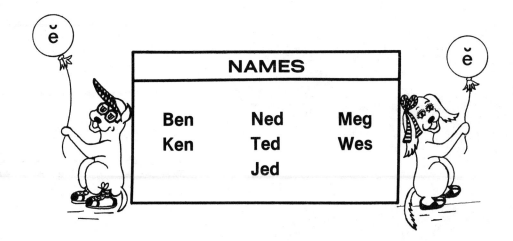

NAMES

Ben	Ned	Meg
Ken	Ted	Wes
	Jed	

RHYMING EGGS

NAME _____

DATE _____

Each nest below has a group of eggs in it.   The eggs have
pictures on them.   Write the words that name the pictures.
Read your rhyming words!

_en   words

hen_____   _____

_____   _____

_eg   words

_____

_____   _____

_et   words

_____

_____

GET THE NET!

Scooter has a fish!
Help the dogs get the net!

NAME _____

DATE _____

🐾 You must run down the dock to get the net from J.J.
Write the word that names each picture along the way.

The Messy Tent of Ed and Ben

NAME _____

Can you find anything?

Check ○ YES or NO.

	YES	NO		YES	NO
Can you find **Ben**?	O	O	Can you find a **pet**?	O	O
Can you find a **pen**?	O	O	Can you find a **web**?	O	O
Can you find a **jet**?	O	O	Can you find a **ten**?	O	O
Can you find a **keg**?	O	O	Can you find two **men**?	O	O
Can you find a **net**?	O	O	Can you find **Ed's leg**?	O	O
Can you find a **bed**?	O	O	Can you find a **nest**?	O	O
Can you find a **hen**?	O	O	Color the things you found!		

18

What's Happening?

NAME_____

DATE_____

Get ready to match sentences with pictures! Each sentence below will tell us what is happening in one of the pictures. Draw lines from sentences to matching pictures. Read carefully!

The men met.

The pet begs.

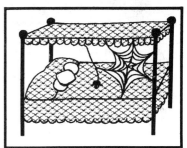

Bess fed her pets.

A web is on the bed.

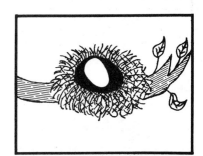

Ted will get wet!

A ten is on a keg.

An egg is in the nest.

He let a hen into the pen.

LET'S TALK ABOUT
the Sound of Short I /i/

Indian

igloo

Words to Read and Spell

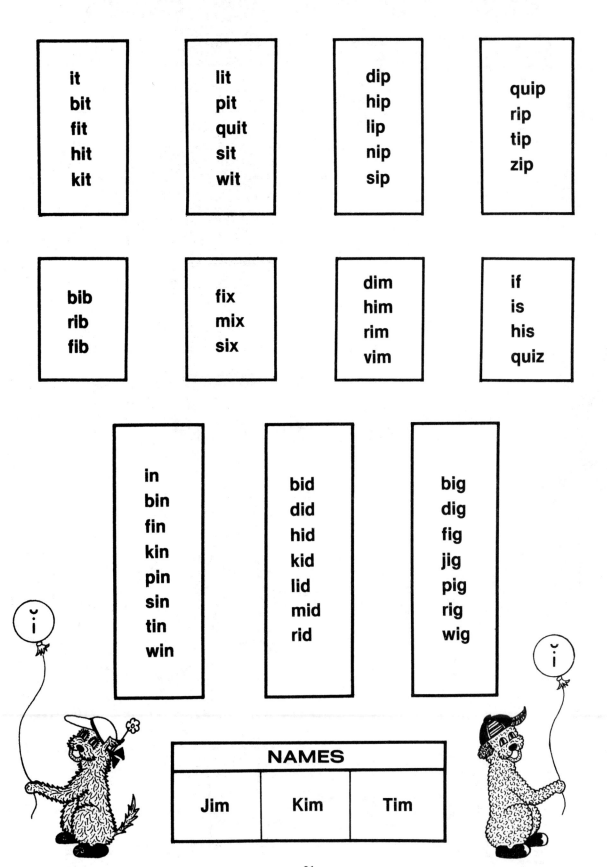

it	lit	dip	quip
bit	pit	hip	rip
fit	quit	lip	tip
hit	sit	nip	zip
kit	wit	sip	

bib	fix	dim	if
rib	mix	him	is
fib	six	rim	his
		vim	quiz

in	bid	big
bin	did	dig
fin	hid	fig
kin	kid	jig
pin	lid	pig
sin	mid	rig
tin	rid	wig
win		

NAMES		
Jim	Kim	Tim

21

Rhyming Grins of Happy Friends

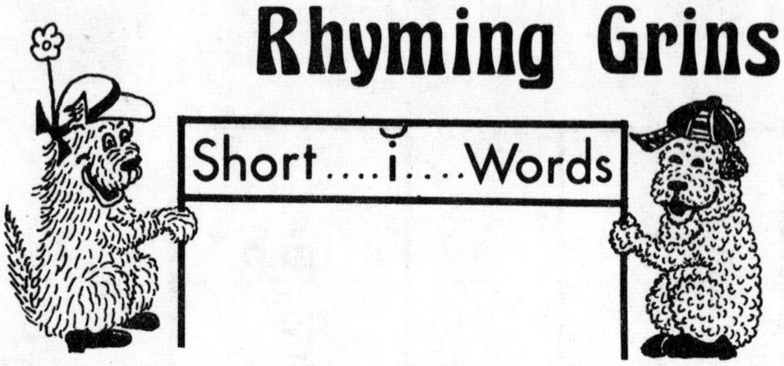

Short....i....Words

NAME_____

DATE_____

The animals below have pictures on their teeth!   Write the word that names each picture.   Read your rhyming words!

dig
_____
_____
_ig words

_ip words
_____
_____

_ix words
_____
_____

_in words
_____
_____

_ib words
_____
_____

22

WELCOME TO DOGTOWN'S
Sixth Street Jig

Come dance to the
Dogtown Jig!

NAME _____

DATE _____

 Dance down Sixth Street with the dogs! Write the word that
names each picture along the way.

23

DINNER WITH A PIG!

NAME_____

Come have dinner with Pig Jiglet! What can you find at his table?

Check ⊘ YES or NO.

	YES	NO
Can you find a **pig**?	○	○
Can you find a **bib**?	○	○
Can you find **figs**?	○	○
Can you find **ribs**?	○	○
Can you find something to **sip**?	○	○

	YES	NO
Can you find a **lid**?	○	○
Can you find a **wig**?	○	○
Can you find a **kit**?	○	○
Can you find a **rip**?	○	○
Can you find a **pin**?	○	○

24

Color the things you found!

What's Happening?

NAME _____

DATE _____

Get ready to match sentences with pictures! Each sentence below will tell us what is happening in one of the pictures. Draw lines from sentences to matching pictures. Read carefully!

Dixie will fix the rip.

It bit him on his hip!

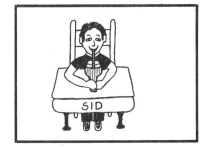

A pin is in his bib.

The pig did a jig!

Sid will sit and sip.

The mitt fits him.

Winston will mix a dip.

If he hits it, he will win!

25

LET'S TALK ABOUT
the Sound of Short O /o/

Words to Read and Spell

dog	cop	cod
fog	hop	mod
hog	mop	nod
log	top	rod
sog	sop	pod
jog	pop	sod
		god

cot	hot	cob
dot	lot	mob
not	rot	rob
got	tot	sob
pot	jot	

bob	ox	on
lob	box	con
job	fox	mom
gob		

NAMES	
Bob	Tom
Don	God
Ron	

DOGGONE EXCEPTIONS	
son	of
ton	
won	

Rhyming BLOCKS

short o words

NAME_____

DATE_____

Each dog below has a stack of blocks. The blocks have pictures on them. Write the words that name the pictures. Read your rhyming words!

_og words

log

_____ _____

_op words

_____ _____ _____

_ot words

_____ _____ _____

_ox words

_____ _____

28

THE ★ DOGTOWN ★ JOG

Come join the dogs
for a jogging race!

NAME _____

DATE _____

 You must jog down the track to the hot dogs and pop!
Write the word that names each picture along the way.

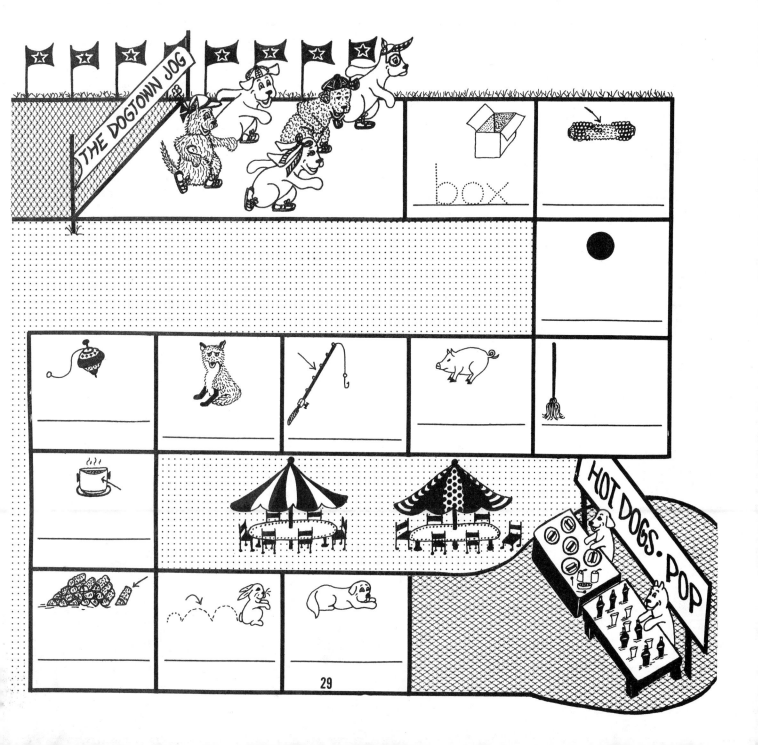

box

_____

29

The Pot Shop of Farmer Tom

NAME _____

Farmer Tom's Pot Shop

What do you see at Farmer Tom's Pot Shop?

Check ✓ YES or NO.

	YES	NO
Do you see **pots**?	O	O
Do you see a **box**?	O	O
Do you see a **cot**?	O	O
Do you see a **mop**?	O	O
Do you see an **ox**?	O	O

	YES	NO
Do you see **logs**?	O	O
Do you see a **fox**?	O	O
Do you see a **hog**?	O	O
Do you see a **rod**?	O	O

 Color the things you saw!

30

What's Happening?

Get ready to match sentences with pictures! Each sentence below will tell us what is happening in one of the pictures. Draw lines from sentences to matching pictures. Read carefully!

Bob got a top!

The logs are hot.

Tom's job is to mop.

The hog is on a cot.

A dot is on the box.

This dog is not hot!

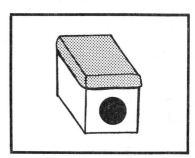

The fox has a rod.

Rob has a lot of pots.

31

LET'S TALK ABOUT
the Sound of Short U /u/

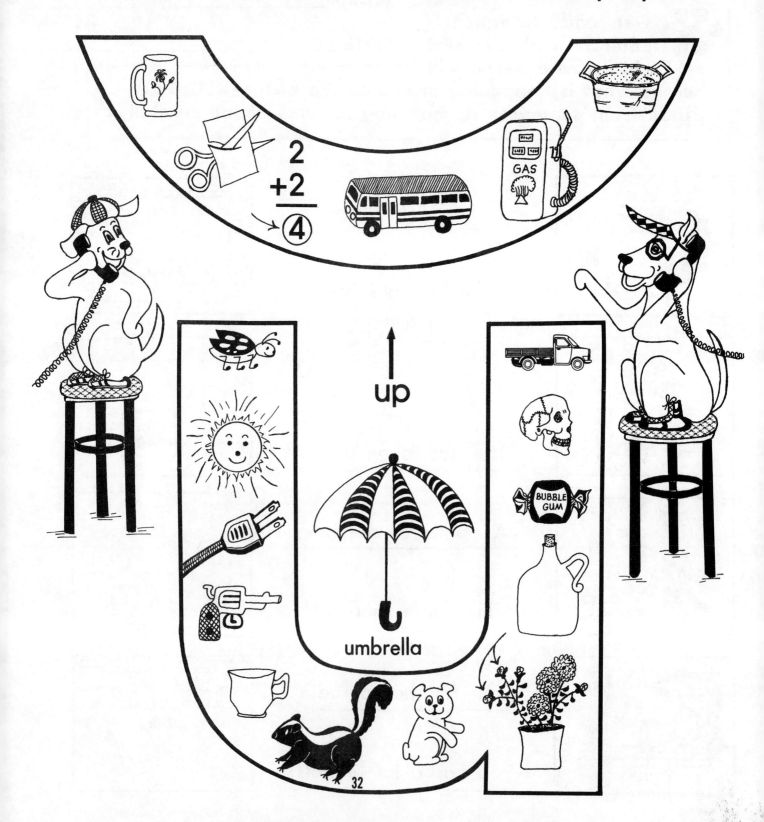

up

umbrella

32

Words to Read and Spell

bug dug hug jug pug	bud cud mud dud	up cup sup pup	mug rug tug lug

but cut hut nut rut gut jut	bun fun nun run sun gun pun	bum hum mum rum sum gum	cub nub rub sub tub pub

us
bus
pus

ŭ

A DOGGONE EXCEPTION

put

ŭ

33

Rhyming Buses

CATCH A RIDE

ON A RHYMING BUS!

NAME_____

DATE_____

Each bus below has a group of pictures on it.   Write the words that name the pictures.   Read your rhyming words!

Tubs and Tubs of Bubbles and Suds

NAME _____

DATE _____

The dogs had too much fun in the mud!
You must help them find Mr. Mutt's Bath Hut!
Write the word that names each picture along the way.

I need a bath!

Start Here

Sun

_____

_____

_____

.....NEED A BATH ?...
MR. MUTT HAS TUBS AND TUBS OF BUBBLES AND SUDS!

_____

_____

2
+2
→④

_____

_____

_____

_____

_____

_____

BUBBLE GUM

ONE WAY

STOP

CLEAN UP AT MR. MUTT'S

Mr. Mutt's Bath Hut

35

The Hut of Uncle Jud

NAME _____

Uncle Jud has a lot of stuff! What can _you_ find in his hut?

Check ✓ YES or NO.

	YES	NO
Can you find a **mug**?	○	○
Can you find a **tub**?	○	○
Can you find 3 **pups**?	○	○
Can you find a **rug**?	○	○
Can you find a **bus**?	○	○
Can you find a **cup**?	○	○

	YES	NO
Can you find a **jug**?	○	○
Can you find a **bud**?	○	○
Can you find a **gun**?	○	○
Can you find a **cub**?	○	○
Can you find a **bug**?	○	○

36 Color the things you found!

What's Happening?

NAME _____

DATE _____

Get ready to match sentences with pictures! Each sentence below will tell us what is happening in one of the pictures. Draw lines from sentences to matching pictures. Read carefully!

The sun is up.

She dug up a nut.

Gum was in this mug!

Russ runs to his hut.

The pup is in a tub.

A bug is on the bud.

Guss will lug his rug.

It's fun to hug a cub!

37

Don't Let Your Words Get Wet!

NAME_____ DATE_____

On every umbrella below, you will see a word ending and four different consonants. Add the word ending to each of the consonants and spell rhyming words! Write your words on the numbered blanks.

_ed   f l r b
1 _____ 3 _____
2 _____ 4 _____

_ot   h r n g
1 _____ 3 _____
2 _____ 4 _____

_ug   d t m h
1 _____ 3 _____
2 _____ 4 _____

_ad   b m s h
1 _____ 3 _____
2 _____ 4 _____

_ip   t s r d
1 _____ 3 _____
2 _____ 4 _____

38

ZAP A VOWEL!

NAME_____ DATE_____

Get ready to zap a vowel! On every game screen below, you will see three pictures. The words that name the pictures have missing vowels. Fill in the right vowels to complete the words...and YOU WILL WIN!

VOWEL ZAPPER!

u a i e

p_n
p_n
p_n

VOWEL ZAPPER!

e u a o

c_p
c_p
c_p

VOWEL ZAPPER!

o a e u

b_g
b_g
b_g

VOWEL ZAPPER!

e o u a

c_t
c_t
c_t

39

Bat for a Vowel and Hit a Home Run!

NAME_____ DATE_____

Welcome to Dogtown's Ball Park! On the baseball diamond, you will see lots of pictures. The words that name the pictures have missing vowels. Fill in the right vowels and hit a home run!

m_p

m_p

g_w

f_n

f_n

f_sh

n_t

n_t

m_n

m_n

l_g

l_g

b_d

b_d

_x

_x

a e i o u

START HERE

40

Aim for a Vowel!

WELCOME TO DOGTOWN'S ARCHERY CONTEST!
To get a perfect score, you must complete all of the words next to the targets. On each target, find and circle 4 vowels that will help you spell the 4 different words.
READY ... AIM ... SHOOT FOR A VOWEL!

NAME_____

DATE_____

h u t
h _ t
h _ t
h _ t

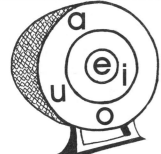

p _ t   p _ t
p _ t   p _ t

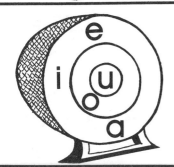

b _ g   b _ g
b _ g   b _ g

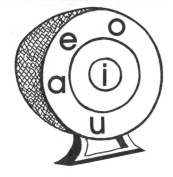

b _ t   b _ t
b _ t   b _ t

41

Ski Vowel Valley!

Come to VOWEL VALLEY and join the dogs for a ski race!

Pick a ski trail. And...
Remember its vowel sound!

YOU WILL NEED : a gameboard (on page 43)
50 game cards (on page 44)
1 announcer
5 ski racers

① Look at the gameboard.   The race begins where you see the dogs. Each racer will ski down a different vowel trail with one of the dogs.

② Cut out the game cards. Put them in a pile, face down.

③ Announcer: Draw a game card. Read the word on it to the ski racers. Don't let the skiers see the word!
Ski Racers: Listen to the vowel sound of the word. The skier, whose trail has that vowel sound, will write the word on the first blank of his/her ski trail.

④ Announcer: Keep drawing and reading the word cards, one at a time. Give the skiers time to write each word.
Ski Racers: Keep moving down VOWEL VALLEY, writing only words that have the vowel sound of your ski trail.

The first skier to write TEN WORDS on a trail
WINS THE VOWEL VALLEY RACE!

Ski Vowel Valley!

ă   ĕ   ĭ   ŏ   ŭ

Ski Vowel Valley!
(Game Cards)

Dear Teacher: After cutting out the cards, you may want to paste them onto larger construction paper squares. The cards will then be easier for your students to handle.

hop	fed	sag	win	fun
tug	rib	job	met	bad
bet	dad	but	nod	rig
sip	hot	leg	sat	mud
mad	hug	sit	yes	mom
got	wet	had	big	rub
fix	lap	rot	van	dip
red	hum	get	lug	fog
tax	rob	hip	peg	up
gut	fit	lot	fat	let

44

A Special Spelling Secret

① When you hear a little word, **listen** carefully.

Does the word have a **short vowel sound?**

/sak/	/lok/	/duk/

lŏk, dŭk, săk... YES! All of these words <u>do</u> have a short vowel sound.

② If the word <u>does</u> have a <u>short vowel sound</u>, **listen** to the **last letter sound** of the word.

sak	lok	duk

The <u>last</u> letter sound I hear is... /<u>k</u>/.

③ If the <u>last letter sound you hear</u> is /k/, you must **WRITE** <u>ck</u> for that last sound **when you SPELL the word:**

sack	lock	duck

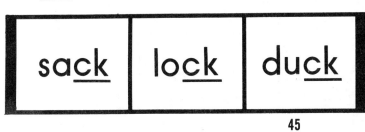

We have written <u>ck</u> for the /k/ sound in sa<u>ck</u>, in lo<u>ck</u> and in du<u>ck</u>. So we now have SPELLED all 3 words correctly!

Words to Read and Spell

back
hack
lack
pack
jack

quack
rack
sack
tack

deck
neck
beck
peck

kick
lick
nick
pick

sick
tick
wick
quick

cock
dock
hock
lock

buck
duck
luck
muck

suck
tuck
puck

sock
rock
mock

ck

ck

NAMES			
Jack Mack	Dick Rick	Nick Vick	Buck Beck

PACK THE SACKS WITH WORDS!

NAME_____ DATE_____

Help the dogs pack the sacks with words that end in <u>ck</u>! On the top of every sack, you will see a list of sound spellings. Write a word for each of the sound spellings. Write your words on the numbered blanks inside the sacks. Read all your words to your teacher!

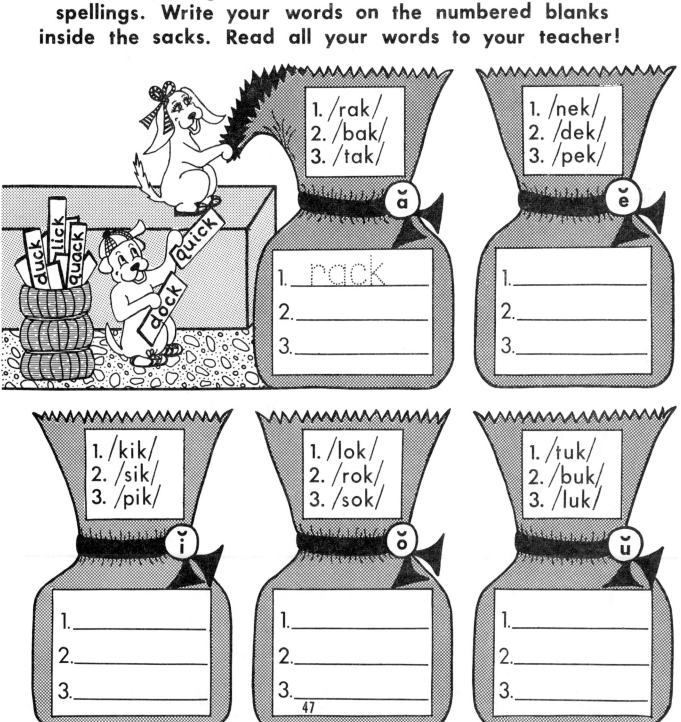

1. /rak/
2. /bak/
3. /tak/

ă

1. pack
2. _____
3. _____

1. /nek/
2. /dek/
3. /pek/

ĕ

1. _____
2. _____
3. _____

1. /kik/
2. /sik/
3. /pik/

ĭ

1. _____
2. _____
3. _____

1. /lok/
2. /rok/
3. /sok/

ŏ

1. _____
2. _____
3. _____

1. /tuk/
2. /buk/
3. /luk/

ŭ

1. _____
2. _____
3. _____

47

Rhyming Hat Racks

NAME_____ DATE_____

On every cap below, you will see a word ending and three different consonants. Add the word ending to each of the consonants and spell rhyming words! Write your words on the numbered blanks.

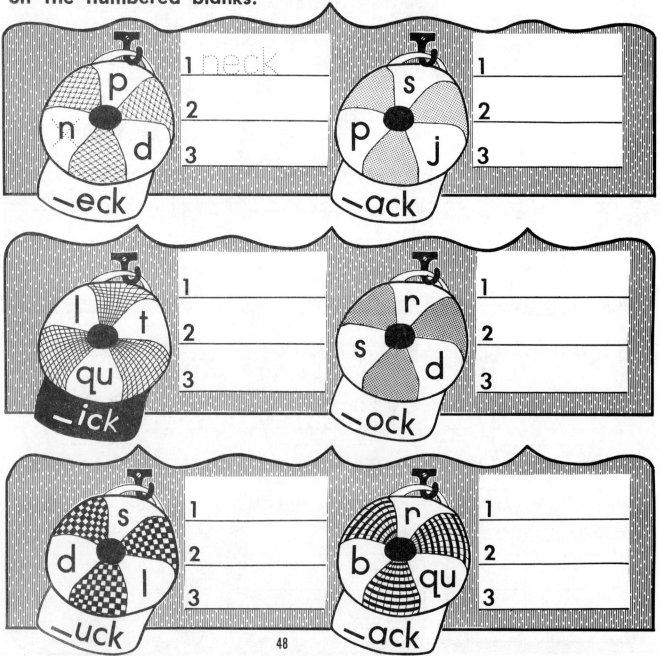

p n d

−eck

1 neck
2
3

s p j

−ack

1
2
3

l t qu

−ick

1
2
3

r s d

−ock

1
2
3

s d l

−uck

1
2
3

r b qu

−ack

1
2
3

48

A Special Spelling Secret

① When you hear a little word, **listen** carefully.

Does the word have a **short vowel sound?**

| puf | hil | mes |

pŭf, hĭl, mĕs...
YES! All of these
words do have a
short
vowel
sound.

② If the word <u>does</u> have a <u>short vowel sound</u>,

listen to the **last letter sound** of the word.

| pu<u>f</u> | hi<u>l</u> | me<u>s</u> |

The <u>last</u>
letter sounds
I hear... are
/<u>f</u>/, /<u>l</u>/ and /<u>s</u>/.

③ If the <u>last letter sound you hear</u> is /f/, /l/, or /s/, you must

<u>**DOUBLE**</u> that last letter when you SPELL the word:

| pu<u>ff</u> | hi<u>ll</u> | me<u>ss</u> |

We DOUBLED the
f in pu<u>ff</u>, the l in
hi<u>ll</u>, and the s in
me<u>ss</u>. So we now
have SPELLED all 3
words <u>correctly</u>!

49

Words to Read and Spell

__ ll Words

ill	mill	sell		dull
bill	pill	tell	bell	hull
fill	sill	well	fell	gull
dill	till	yell	hell	
hill	will	jell	dell	
kill	quill			doll
gill				

__ ss Words

bass	boss	hiss	cuss	less
pass	moss	kiss	fuss	mess
mass	loss	miss	muss	
lass	toss			

__ ff Words

buff
cuff
huff
muff
puff
off

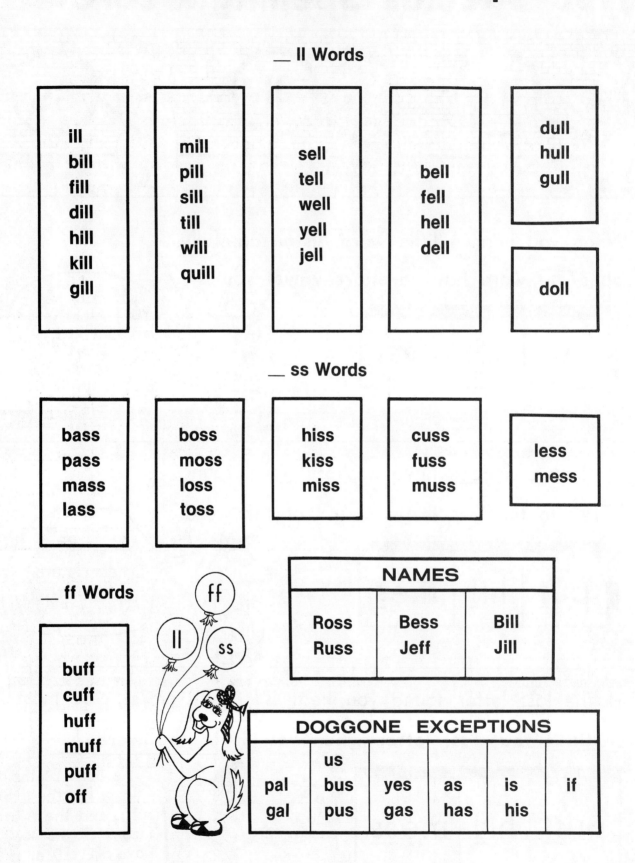

NAMES

Ross	Bess	Bill
Russ	Jeff	Jill

DOGGONE EXCEPTIONS

	us				
pal	bus	yes	as	is	if
gal	pus	gas	has	his	

50

FILL THE WELLS WITH WORDS!

NAME_____ DATE_____

Help the dogs fill the wells with words that end in **ff**, **ll**, or **ss**! On the roof of every well, you will see a list of sound spellings. Write a word for each of the sound spellings. Write your words on the numbered blanks inside the wells. Read all your words to your teacher!

1. /buf/
2. /muf/
3. /puf/

1. buff
2._____
3._____

1. /wil/
2. /hil/
3. /kil/

1._____
2._____
3._____

1. /bas/
2. /mas/
3. /pas/

1._____
2._____
3._____

1. /fel/
2. /tel/
3. /yel/

1._____
2._____
3._____

1. /bos/
2. /tos/
3. /mos/

1._____
2._____
3._____

51

Catch a Rhyming Bass!

NAME_____ DATE_____

On the fins of every bass below, you will see a word ending and several consonants. Add the word ending to each of the consonants and spell rhyming words! Write your words on the numbered blanks.

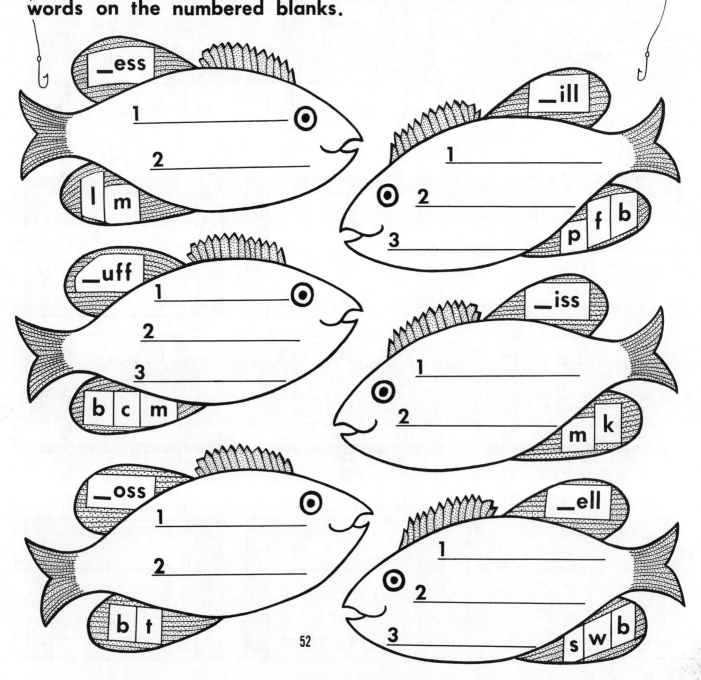

_ess

1 _____
2 _____

l m

_ill

1 _____
2 _____
3 _____

p f b

_uff

1 _____
2 _____
3 _____

b c m

_iss

1 _____
2 _____

m k

_oss

1 _____
2 _____

b t

_ell

1 _____
2 _____
3 _____

s w b

52

TOUCHDOWN

Kick, Pass, or Run for It!

★-★
Come join the dogs for a READING GAME of FOOTBALL!
★-★

YOU WILL NEED : 2 football players
2 gameboard markers
a gameboard (on page 54)
14 KICK cards (on page 55)
14 PASS cards (on page 56)
16 RUN cards (on page 57)

The first Player to reach the TOUCHDOWN space, will WIN the READING FOOTBALL GAME!

① Look at the gameboard. Two football players will race down the field for a TOUCHDOWN! They will KICK, PASS, or RUN FOR IT!

② Look at the game cards. The KICK cards show words that are spelled with ck. The PASS cards show words that end in ff, ll, or ss. The RUN cards show sentences. Cut out all the cards. Put them in 3 piles, face down, on the appropriate gameboard boxes.

③ Player #1: Put your marker on the first KICK space. Draw a KICK card. Read all the words you see. Player #2 will check you. If you read the words correctly, COUNT THE STARS on your card and move ahead that many spaces. If you do NOT read the words correctly, STAY where you are; you will draw another card from the same deck on your next turn. Player #2: Now you do the same.

④ Take turns moving down the gameboard. If your marker is on a KICK space, draw and read a KICK card. If you land on a PASS space, draw and read a PASS card. If you are on a RUN space, draw and read a RUN card.

⬤ TOUCHDOWN ⬤
Kick, Pass, or Run for It!
(Kick Cards)

sick sack sock ★ suck ★	Dick duck dock ★ deck ★	tick tock tack ★ tuck ★
lick lack lock ★ luck ★	pack peck pick ★ puck ★	hack back sack ★ jack ★
kick wick sick pick ★	hock rock sock cock ★	duck luck suck buck ★
Rick rack rock ★	deck neck peck ★	racket jacket packet ★ ★
quick quack ★	rocket pocket ★	

◆ TOUCHDOWN ◆
Kick, Pass, or Run for It!
(Pass Cards)

huff hill hiss ★	puff pill pass ★	muff mill moss ★
buff bell boss ★ ★	Bess boss bass ★ ★	fell fill fuss ★ ★
less loss lass ★ ★	kill kiss cuff ★	bill bass buff ★
well yell tell ★	sell sill sass ★ ★	Jeff cuff off ★
miss mess moss ★ mass ★	dill doll dell ★ dull ★	

56

TOUCHDOWN
Kick, Pass, or Run for It!
(Run Cards)

A rock is on the dock. ★	Bess will kiss the doll. ★	Mack will miss his boss. ★	Rick is not well. He is sick. ★
Jeff fell off the deck! ★ ★	A sock is in the sack. ★	Mr. Muff will sell the mill. ★	He will kick and buck you off! ★ ★
Jack will pick up the mess. ★ ★	Tell Ross to pack his bag. ★ ★	The duck ran up the hill. ★	Nick will pack his sack. ★
The duck will yell, "Quack! Quack!" ★ ★	The dog had a tick on his back. ★		
Bill has a cut on his neck. ★	Dick sells locks and bells. ★ ★		

57

Beginning Consonant Blends

2 consonant sounds at the beginning of a word

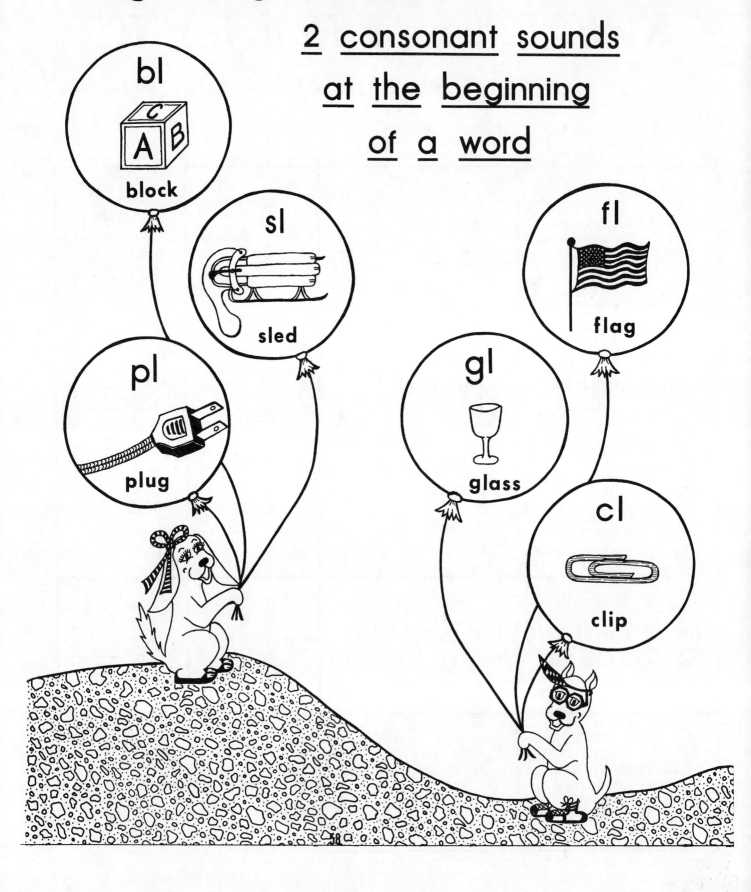

bl — block

sl — sled

pl — plug

fl — flag

gl — glass

cl — clip

Words to Read and Spell

fl	sl	cl	pl	bl	gl
flab	slab	clam	plan	blab	glad
flack	slack	clan	plat	black	glass
flat	slam	clad			glen
flax	slat	class	pled	bled	
flag	slap	clap		bless	gloss
flap			plod		
	sled	click	plot	bliss	glum
fled		cliff	plop		glut
fleck	slick	clip		blob	
flex	slid		pluck	block	
	slim	clock	plum	blot	
flick	slit	clod	plus		
flip	slip	clot	plug		
		clog		bluff	
flock	slot				
floss	slop	club			
flop		cluck			
	slug				
fluff	slum				
flux					

Plug in a Consonant Blend!

NAME_____

DATE_____

Help the dogs plug in a blend! Every plug below has a picture on it. The **name** of each picture will **begin** with **sl**, **pl**, or **bl**. **Circle** the beginning consonant blend for every picture.

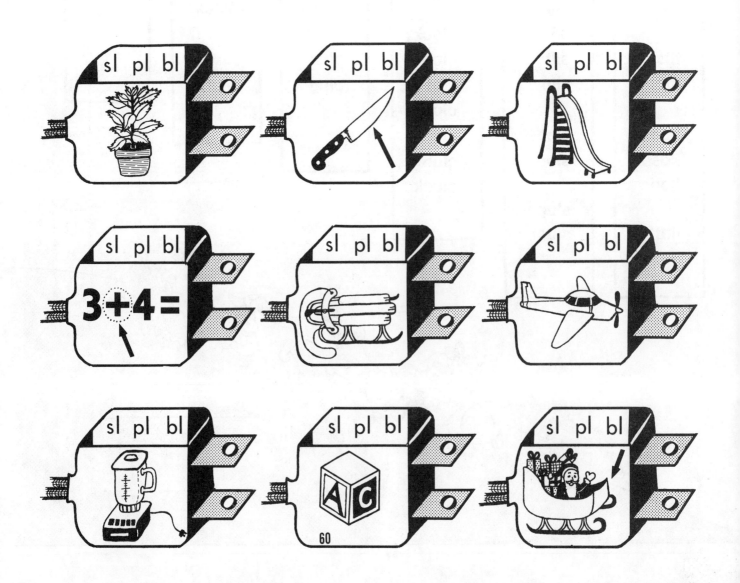

60

Flag Down a Consonant Blend!

NAME_____

DATE_____

Help the dogs flag down a blend! Every flag below has a picture on it. The __name__ of each picture will __begin__ with __fl__, __gl__, or __cl__. __Circle__ the beginning consonant blend for every picture.

Fill a Glass with Rhyming Words!

NAME_____ DATE_____

On each glass below, you will see a word ending. There are two consonant blends on every lemon slice. Add the word ending to each of the consonant blends and spell rhyming words! Write your words on the numbered blanks inside the glasses.

Read all your words to your teacher!

pl sl
1. plot
2.
_ot

cl fl
1.
2.
_ap

bl fl
1.
2.
_uff

cl sl
1.
2.
_ick

fl pl
1.
2.
_op

sl bl
1.
2.
_ack

pl sl
1.
2.
_ug

fl sl
1.
2.
_ip

sl bl
1.
2.
_ed

gl cl
1.
2.
_ass

cl bl
1.
2.
_ock

Mr. Black's Happy Class

NAME_____

	Check ✓ YES or NO.

What will <u>you</u> see in Mr. Black's class?

	YES	NO		YES	NO
Will you see a **clock?**	○	○	Will you see a **flag?**	○	○
Will you see a **plug?**	○	○	Will you see **blocks?**	○	○
Will you see a **sled?**	○	○	Will you see a **plus?**	○	○
Will you see a **clip?**	○	○	Will you see a **class?**	○	○
Will you see a **black cat?**	○	○			

63

 Color the things you saw!

The Vowel-Cliff-Glasses Hunt

VOWEL CLIFF → →

Come to VOWEL CLIFF and help the dogs find Scooter's glasses!

My glasses! I _dropped_ my glasses!

They must be at the bottom of VOWEL CLIFF!

Pick a ladder. And... remember its vowel sound!

YOU WILL NEED : a gameboard (on page 65)
30 game cards (on page 66)
1 announcer
5 cliff climbers

1. Look at the gameboard. There are five ladders on VOWEL CLIFF. Each cliff climber will move down a ladder with one of the dogs.

2. Cut out the game cards. Put them in a pile, face down.

3. Announcer: Draw a game card. Read the word on it to the cliff climbers. Don't let them see the word!
Cliff Climbers: Listen to the <u>vowel sound</u> of the word. The climber whose ladder has that vowel sound will <u>write the word</u> on the first step of his/her ladder.

4. Announcer: Keep drawing and reading word cards, one at a time. Give the climbers time to write each word.
Cliff Climbers: Keep moving down VOWEL CLIFF, writing only words that have the vowel sound of <u>your</u> ladder.

<u>WHO</u> WILL FIND SCOOTER'S GLASSES???
The first cliff climber to write SIX words on a ladder!

The Vowel-Cliff-Glasses Hunt

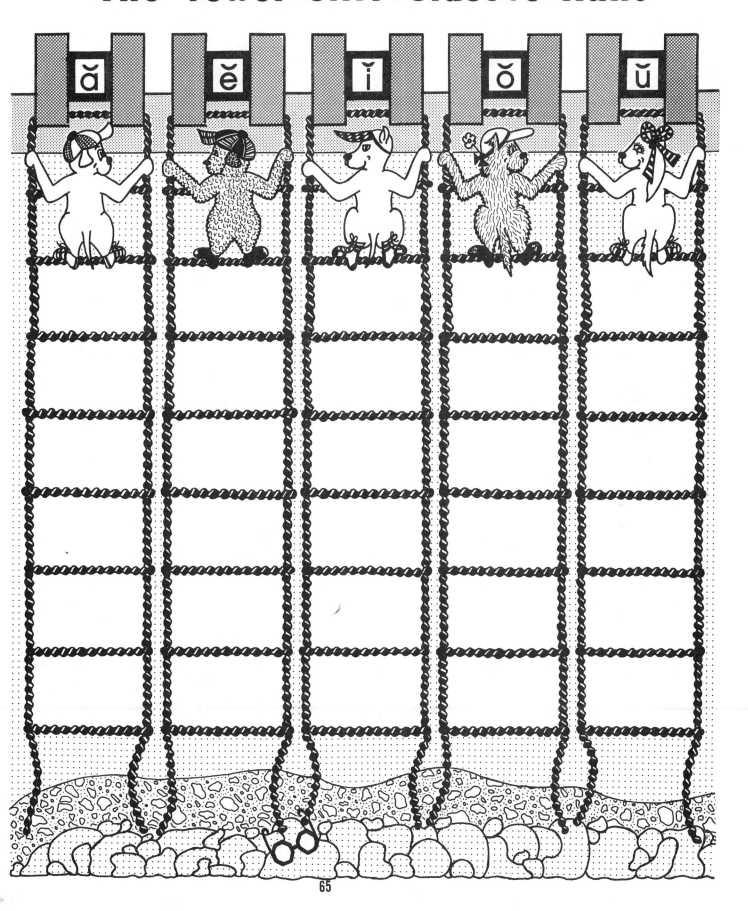

The Vowel-Cliff-Glasses Hunt

(Game Cards)

plum	block	slim	plan	flop
bless	flag	click	club	slot
glad	clip	sled	plop	fluff
slid	bled	clod	slam	plug
clock	slug	flat	Glen	flip
fled	clam	slip	flex	bluff

Beginning Consonant Blends

2 consonant sounds at the beginning of a word

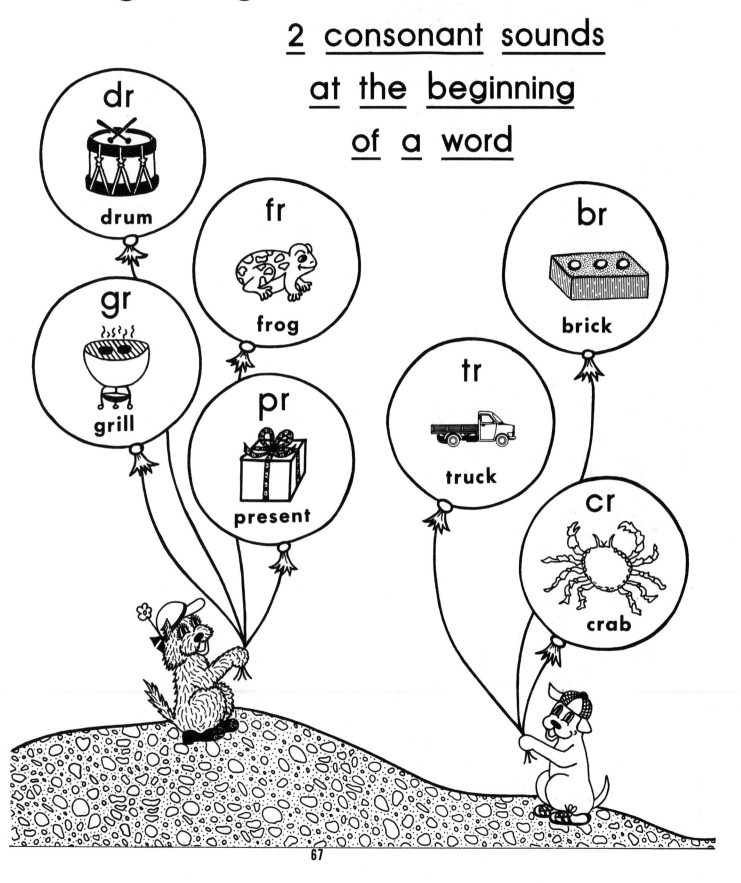

dr — drum

fr — frog

br — brick

gr — grill

pr — present

tr — truck

cr — crab

Words to Read and Spell

gr	br	tr	cr
grab	brad	track	crab
gram	bran	tram	crack
grass	brass	trap	cram
	brat		
Greg	brag	trick	crib
		trim	crick
grid	bred	trip	
grim	Bret		crock
grin		trod	cross
grit	brick	trot	crop
grill	brim		
grip		truck	crux
grog			
grub			
gruff			

dr	pr	fr
drab	press	Fran
drag	prep	
dress	prick	Fred
	prim	fret
drill		frill
drip	prod	
drop	prom	from
	prop	frog
drug		
drum		

The Consonant-Blend Parachute Drop

NAME_____ DATE_____

Welcome to the **DOGTOWN PARACHUTE DROP!** Every parachute below has a picture on it. The <u>name</u> of each picture will <u>begin</u> with <u>fr</u>, <u>dr</u>, or <u>gr</u>. <u>Circle</u> the beginning consonant blend for every picture.

Cross the Tracks with a Consonant Blend!

NAME_____ DATE_____

Welcome to the **DOGTOWN TRAIN STATION!**
Every train below has a picture on it. The <u>name</u>
of each picture will <u>begin</u> with <u>br</u>, <u>tr</u>, <u>cr</u>, or <u>pr</u>. <u>Circle</u>
the beginning consonant blend for every picture.

Rhyming Trucks

NAME_____ DATE_____

Fill the trucks with rhyming words! On the doors of every truck below, you will see a word ending and a list of consonant blends. Add the word ending to each consonant blend and spell rhyming words! Write your words on the numbered blanks. Read all your words to your teacher.

_ack | tr cr | 1. track 2. _____

_ill | dr gr | 1. _____ 2. _____

_ab | cr gr | 1. _____ 2. _____

_im | br tr | 1. _____ 2. _____

_ess | dr pr | 1. _____ 2. _____

_op | dr cr | 1. _____ 2. _____

_ip | tr gr | 1. _____ 2. _____

_ick | br tr | 1. _____ 2. _____

_ag | dr br | 1. _____ 2. _____

_ass | br gr | 1. _____ 2. _____

71

Grab That Frog!

gr   dr   fr   pr

Welcome to the DOGTOWN FROG GRAB !

Pick a lane on the race track. And remember its beginning consonant blend!

YOU WILL NEED : a gameboard (on page 73)
24 game cards (on page 74)
1 announcer
4 frog grabbers

① Look at the gameboard. The race begins where you see the dogs. Each frog grabber will run down a different racetrack lane with one of the dogs.

② Cut out the game cards. Put them in a pile, face down.

③ Announcer: Draw a game card. Read the word on it to the frog grabbers. Don't let them see the word!
Frog Grabbers: Listen to the <u>beginning</u> <u>consonant</u> <u>sounds</u> of the word. The frog grabber whose lane has that sound will <u>write the word</u> on the first blank of his/her lane.

④ Announcer: Keep drawing and reading the word cards, one at a time. Give the frog grabbers time to write each word.
Frog Grabbers: Keep moving down the racetrack, writing only words that have the beginning sound of your lane.

The first frog grabber to write <u>six</u> <u>words</u> on a lane
<u>WINS</u> the DOGTOWN FROG GRAB!

Grab That Frog!

gr

dr

fr

pr

Grab That Frog!

Word Cards

grass	drum	Fred	press
drag	Fran	prop	grab
from	prick	grip	drug
prom	frog	drip	grill
drop	gruff	prim	fret
grin	prep	frill	drill

TRAP THAT RAT!

Welcome to the DOGTOWN RAT RACE!

YOU WILL NEED : a gameboard (on page 76)
18 game cards (on page 77)
1 announcer
3 rat trappers

Pick a racing platform. And remember its beginning consonant blend!

① Look at the gameboard. There are three racing platforms. Each rat trapper will move along a different platform with one of the dogs. Get ready to trap that rat!

② Cut out the game cards. Put them in a pile, face down.

③ <u>Announcer:</u> Draw a game card. Read the word on it to the rat trappers. Don't let them see the word!
<u>Rat Trappers:</u> Listen to the <u>beginning</u> <u>consonant</u> <u>sounds</u> of the word. The rat trapper whose platform has that sound will <u>write the word</u> on any blank of his/her racing platform.

④ <u>Announcer:</u> Keep drawing and reading the word cards, one at a time. Give the rat trappers time to write each word.
<u>Rat Trappers:</u> Keep moving along your racing platforms. Write only words that have the beginning sound of <u>your</u> platform.

The first rat trapper to write <u>six words</u> on a platform
<u>WINS</u> the DOGTOWN RAT RACE!

TRAP THAT RAT!

TRAP THAT RAT!
Game Cards

brag	crab	trap
crib	trip	brass
trot	brim	crop
brat	cross	trim
cram	trick	brick
truck	brad	crack

77

A PICNIC WITH FRAN AND FRED

NAME_____

 Check ✓ YES or NO.

Come have a picnic with Fran and Fred! What will _you_ see at the park?

	YES	NO
Will you see a **grill**?	◯	◯
Will you see a **drum**?	◯	◯
Will you see a **crab**?	◯	◯
Will you see a **frog**?	◯	◯
Will you see **Fran**?	◯	◯

	YES	NO
Will you see **grass**?	◯	◯
Will you see **bricks**?	◯	◯
Will you see a **crib**?	◯	◯
Will you see a **truck**?	◯	◯
Will you see a **cross**?	◯	◯
Will you see a **track**?	◯	◯

The Dogtown Croquet Classic

YOU WILL NEED : a croquet partner (2 players)
a gameboard (on page 80)
30 game cards (on pages 81 and 82)
2 gameboard markers (on page 82)

① Look at the gameboard. The croquet players will race up the course to the DOGTOWN LODGE. Get ready to hit your croquet balls through the hoops!

② Look at the game cards. Each card has a question on it. Cut out all the cards. Put them in a pile, face down, on the gameboard.

③ Cut out the gameboard markers. Place them on the START space.

④ Player #1: Draw a game card. Read the question you see and answer it. Player #2 will check you. If the answer to your question is "YES," COUNT THE BALLS on the card and move ahead that many spaces. If the answer to your question is "NO," DO NOT count the balls on the card. Instead, you will move backwards to the nearest croquet hoop. Player #2: Now you do the same.

⑤ Take turns moving along the croquet course. If you run out of game cards, mix the deck and keep drawing. The first player to reach the DOGTOWN LODGE WINS the DOGTOWN CROQUET CLASSIC!

The Dogtown Croquet Classic

DOGTOWN LODGE

START HERE

Game Cards

80

The Dogtown Croquet Classic
(Game Cards)

Will Fran grin if she is sad ?	Can you plug in a crock pot ?	Can a rock slip off a cliff ?	Can a hat have a brim ?	Can a truck cross a track ?	Can a bun get hot on a grill ?
Can a clock have a plug ?	Can a drum pick a plum ?	Can a glad mom brag ?	Can a trap trick a rat ?	Can you plan a trip ?	Can you press a dress ?
Can you trip on a slick rock ?	Can a clip slug a sled ?	Can a clam slam on a bug ?	Will Brad grin if he is glad ?	Can a block slap and grab ?	Can you slip on wet grass ?

The Dogtown Croquet Classic
(Game Cards)

Can you dress a doll ?	Can you drag a sled ?
Will a crib flip ?	Can a flag flap ?
Can a frog hop ?	Can a class clap ?
Can a drip drop ?	Can you trim grass ?
Can a glass crack ?	Can a crab dig ?
Can a brick get mad ?	Can you grab a black brick ?

Game Markers

Beginning Consonant Blends

2 consonant sounds
at the beginning
of a word

sn
sniff

sp
spill

sw
swim

sk
skull

st
stop

sm
smoke

Words to Read and Spell

st	sp	sn	sm	sw	sk
stab	span	snack	smack	swag	skid
stack	spat	snap		swam	skiff
staff			smell		skill
stag	speck	sniff		swell	skim
Stan	sped	snip	smock		skin
	spell		smog	swig	skit
stem		snob		swim	skip
step	spill		smug	Swiss	
	spin	snub	smut		
stick	spit	snuff			
stiff		snug			
still	spot				
stock	spud				
stop	spun				

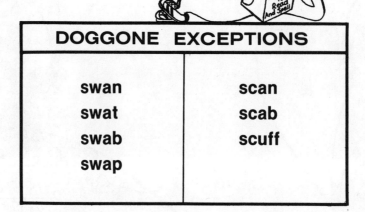

DOGGONE EXCEPTIONS	
swan	scan
swat	scab
swab	scuff
swap	

Spin the Tops with a Consonant Blend

NAME_____

DATE_____

Help the dogs spin their tops with consonant blends! Every top on this page has a picture. The __name__ of each picture will __begin__ with __sp__, __sk__, or __sm__. __Circle__ the beginning consonant blend for every picture.

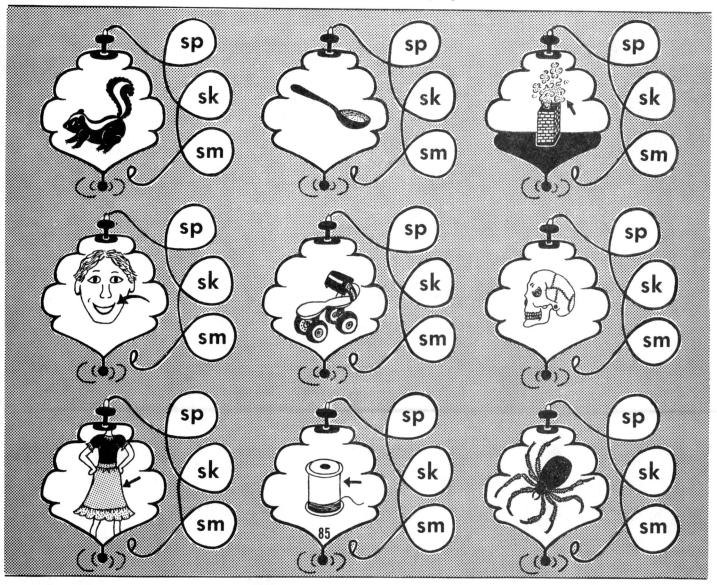

Stop for a Consonant Blend!

STOP

STOP

NAME_____

DATE_____

Can you STOP for a consonant blend?

Every stop sign below has a picture on it. The __name__ of each picture will __begin__ with __sn__, __st__, or __sw__. __Circle__ the beginning consonant blend for every picture.

86

Rhyming Stems

NAME_____ DATE_____

In the center of every flower, you will see a word ending. On the flower petals, you will see beginning consonant blends. Add the **right** consonant blends to the word endings and spell rhyming words! Write your words on the numbered stems of each flower.

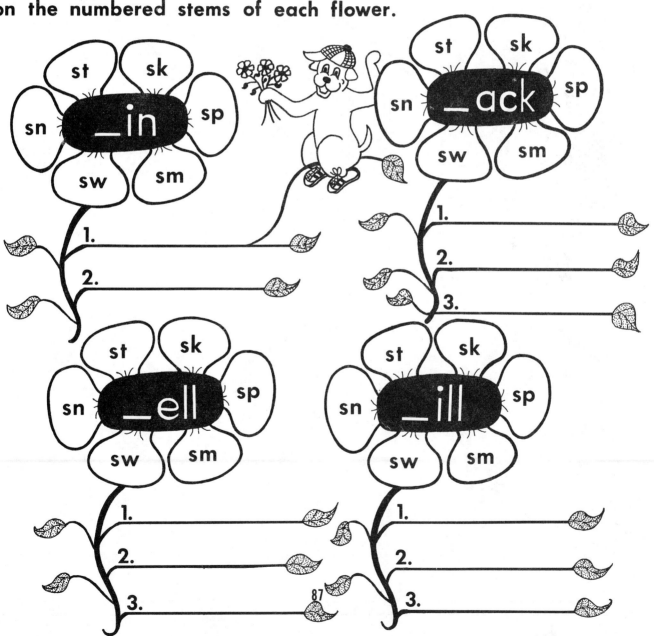

Step Up to a Vowel!

NAME_____ DATE_____

🐾 On every doghouse below, you will see a word with a missing vowel. Step up and find the vowels that can be used to complete the words! Spell two different words by using two different vowels. Write your words on the numbered steps.

st _ p
a e i o u
1.
2.

sp _ t
a e i o u
1.
2.

sk _ ll
a e i o u
1.
2.

st _ ck
a e i o u
1.
2.

st _ ff
a e i o u
1.
2.

sw _ m
a e i o u
1.
2.

BOWL FOR A CONSONANT BLEND

Spell with Skill and Smack ten pins!

 YOU WILL NEED : 5 bowlers
1 scorekeeper
a gameboard (on page 91)
30 game cards (on page 92)
crayons or colored pencils

① Look at the gameboard. There are five bowling lanes.
<u>Bowlers:</u> Pick a lane and remember its vowel sound.
Get ready to spell with skill and smack ten pins!

② Cut out the game cards. Put them in a pile, face down.

③ <u>Scorekeeper:</u> Draw a game card. Read the word on it
to the bowlers. Don't let them see the word!

Turn <u>the page</u>
for more
instructions.

BOWL FOR A CONSONANT BLEND

④ <u>Bowlers</u>: Listen to the <u>vowel sound</u> of the word. The bowler whose lane has that vowel sound will <u>write the word</u> in the first box of his / her lane. If the word is spelled correctly, you will take the card from the scorekeeper. COUNT THE BOWLING PINS on the card and COLOR that number of pins, in your lane, on the gameboard.

If the word you write is <u>NOT</u> spelled correctly, the scorekeeper will let you see and study the word card. DO NOT color any pins on the gameboard. ERASE your misspelled word and give the game card back to the scorekeeper. The scorekeeper will put this card into the middle of the deck; it will be drawn again later.

⑤ <u>Scorekeeper:</u> Continue to draw and read the game cards, one at a time. Give the bowlers time to write each word.

<u>Bowlers</u>: Keep moving up the bowling lanes. Write only words that have the vowel sound of your lane. On each turn, color only the number of pins that you have counted on a card.

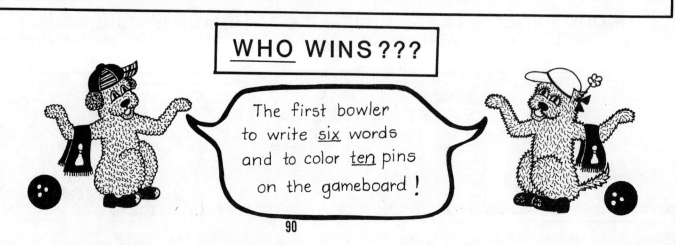

WHO WINS ???

The first bowler
to write <u>six</u> words
and to color <u>ten</u> pins
on the gameboard !

BOWL FOR A CONSONANT BLEND!

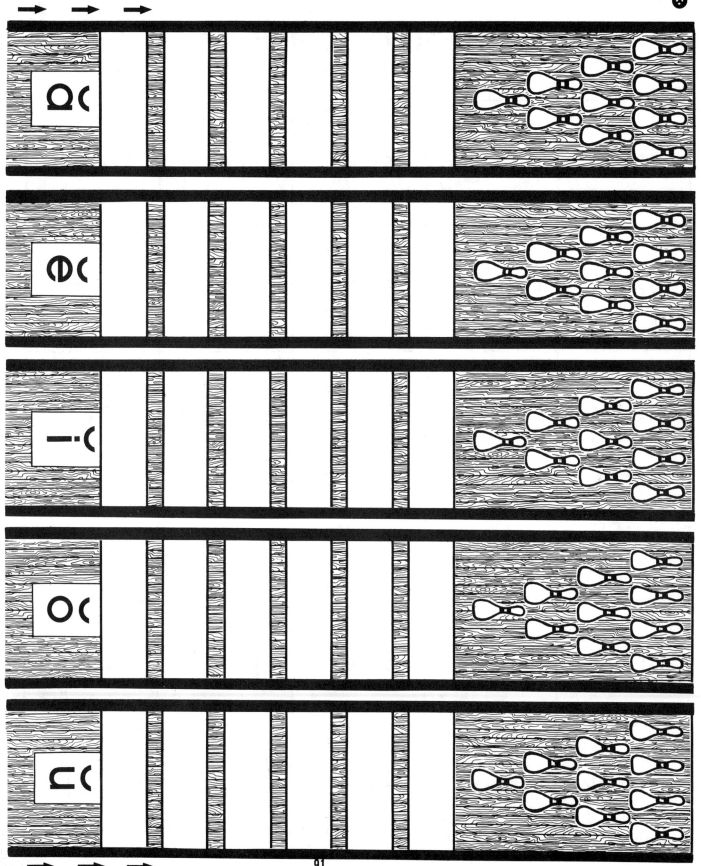

BOWL FOR A CONSONANT BLEND!
(game cards)

smell	snug	stop	spin	swam
swim	smack	skull	stem	spot
stack	skip	spell	smock	spun
sniff	step	stuff	snap	stock
snob	stuck	stab	speck	still
snack	smog	swell	stick	snuff

LET'S TALK ABOUT
the Sound of Ch

cherry

LET'S TALK ABOUT
the Sound of Sh

shell

LET'S TALK ABOUT
the Sound of Th

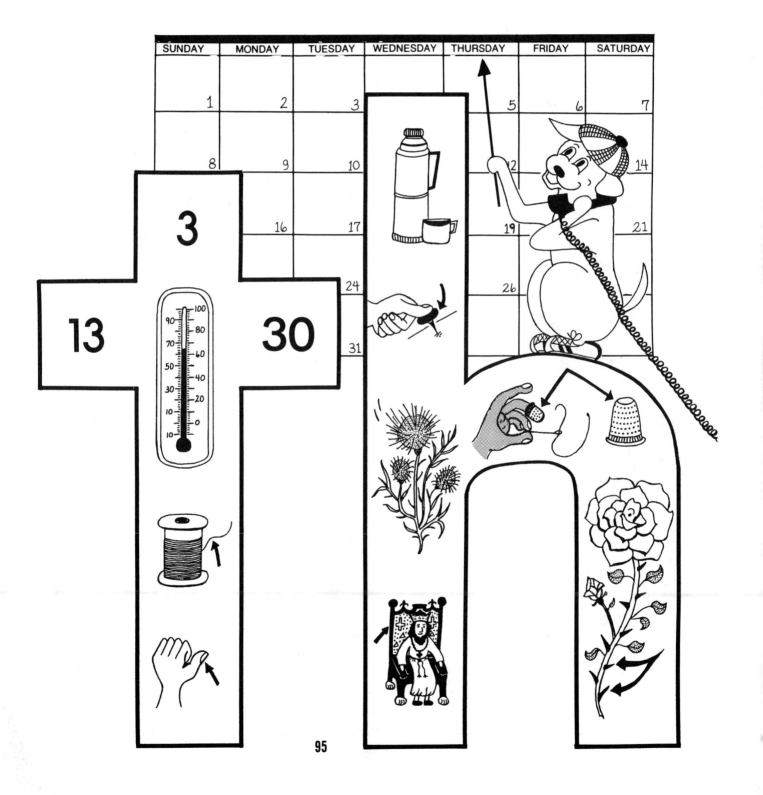

LET'S TALK ABOUT
the Sound of Wh

Consonant Digraphs

2 consonants
that make
1 special sound
at the beginning
of a word

sh — ship

wh — whip

ch — chin

th — thin

Words to Read and Spell

sh	ch	th	_th_	wh
shack	Chad	thar		whack
shad	chaff	that		
shall	chat			when
sham	chap	them		whet
shag		then		
	check			whiff
shed	chess	this		whim
shell				whit
	chick	thus		whiz
shin	chill			whip
ship	chin			
	chip	thick		
shock		thin		
shod	chop			
shot		thud		
shop	Chuck	thug		
	chum			
shuck	chug			
shun				
shut				

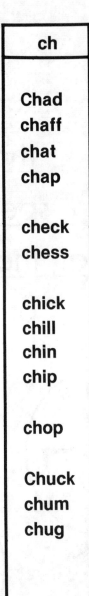

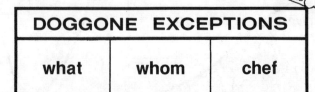

DOGGONE EXCEPTIONS		
what	whom	chef

98

Shuck a Cob!

NAME_____

DATE_____

Every cob below has a picture on it. The <u>name</u> of each picture will <u>begin</u> with <u>sh</u>, <u>ch</u>, <u>wh</u>, or <u>th</u>. <u>Circle</u> the beginning consonant digraph for every picture.

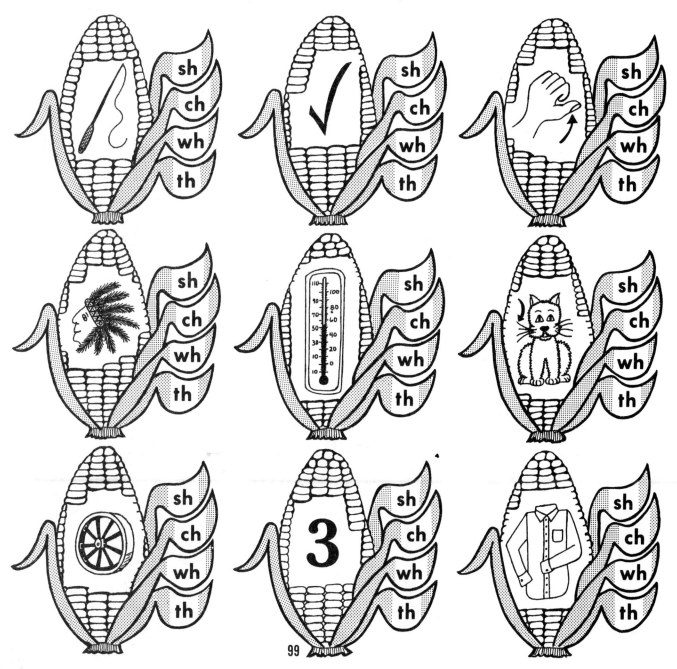

Chop a Log!

NAME_____

DATE_____

Every hatchet below has a picture on it. The **name** of each picture will **begin** with **sh**, **ch**, **wh**, or **th**. **Circle** the beginning consonant digraph for every picture.

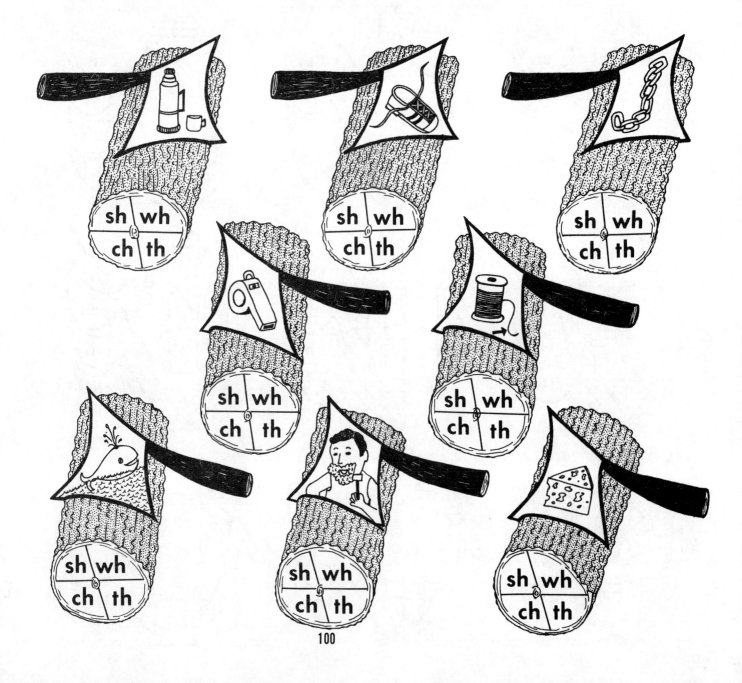

RHYMING SHELLS

On the top of every shell, you will see a word ending. On the bottom of every shell, you will see consonant digraphs. Add the **right** consonant digraphs to the word endings and spell rhyming words! Write your words on the numbered blanks.

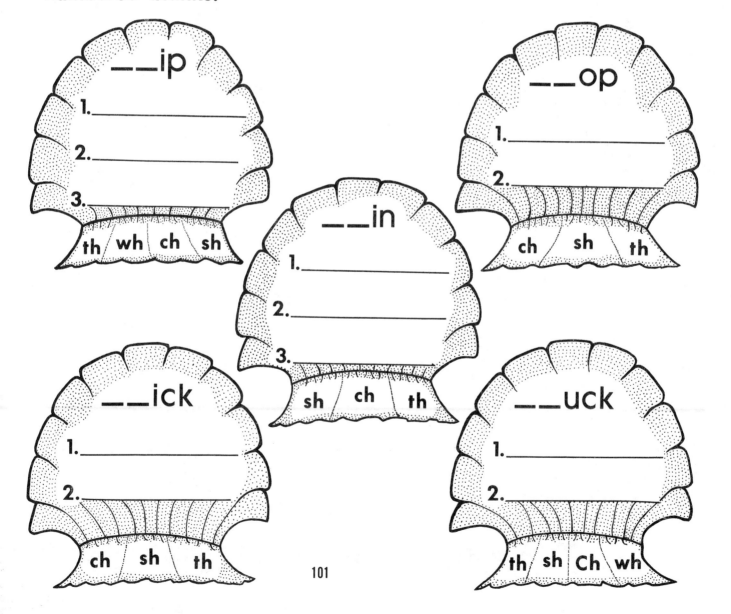

__ip

1._____
2._____
3._____

th / wh / ch / sh

__op

1._____
2._____

ch / sh / th

__in

1._____
2._____
3._____

sh / ch / th

__ick

1._____
2._____

ch / sh / th

__uck

1._____
2._____

th / sh / Ch / wh

101

Check a Chick for Missing Vowels!

NAME_____ **DATE**_____

Please help the dog doctors! The chicks are sick and they need <u>your</u> vowels to get well. You must find and fill in the right vowels to complete two different words on every chick.

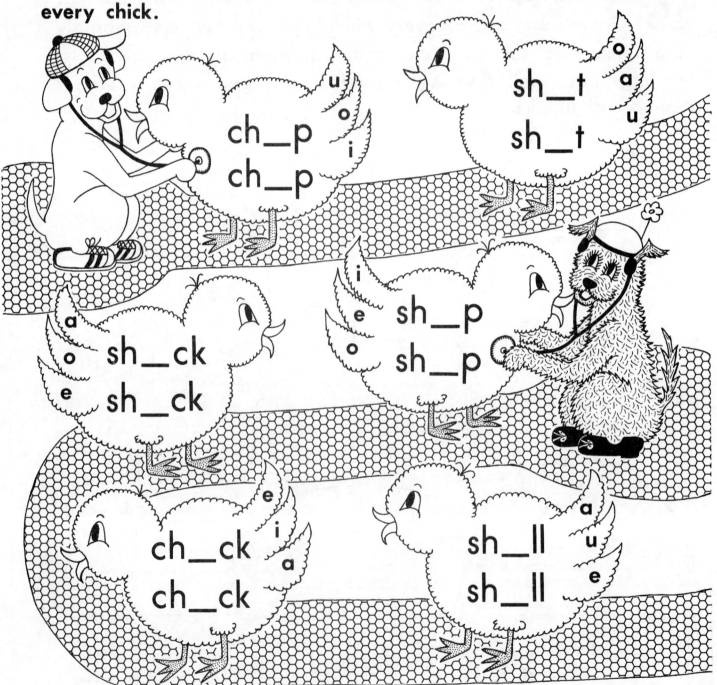

ch_p
ch_p
u o i

sh_t
sh_t
o a u

sh_ck
sh_ck
a o e

sh_p
sh_p
i e o

ch_ck
ch_ck
e i a

sh_ll
sh_ll
a u e

CATCH THAT WOODCHUCK!

Help the dogs get Dixie's keys!

YOU WILL NEED: 2 runners
a gameboard (on page 104)
34 game cards (on pages 105 and 106)
2 gameboard markers

1. Look at the gameboard.   The runners will race down the Tunnel Road to get Dixie's keys from that wood-chuck! There are 20 spaces on the road. You will count each tunnel as one space. Get ready to catch that woodchuck!

2. Look at the game cards. Each card has a question on it. Cut out all the game cards. Put them in a pile, face down, on the gameboard.

3. Place your game markers on the START space.

4. Runner # 1: Draw a game card. Read the question you see and answer it. Runner # 2 will check you. If the answer to your question is "YES," COUNT THE KEYS on the card and move ahead that many spaces. If the answer to your question is "NO," DO NOT count the keys on the card. Instead you will stay where you are until your next turn. Player # 2: Now you do the same.

5. Take turns moving along Tunnel Road.
   The first runner to reach the woodchuck …
   will get to shop FREE at DIXIE'S!!!

CATCH THAT WOODCHUCK!

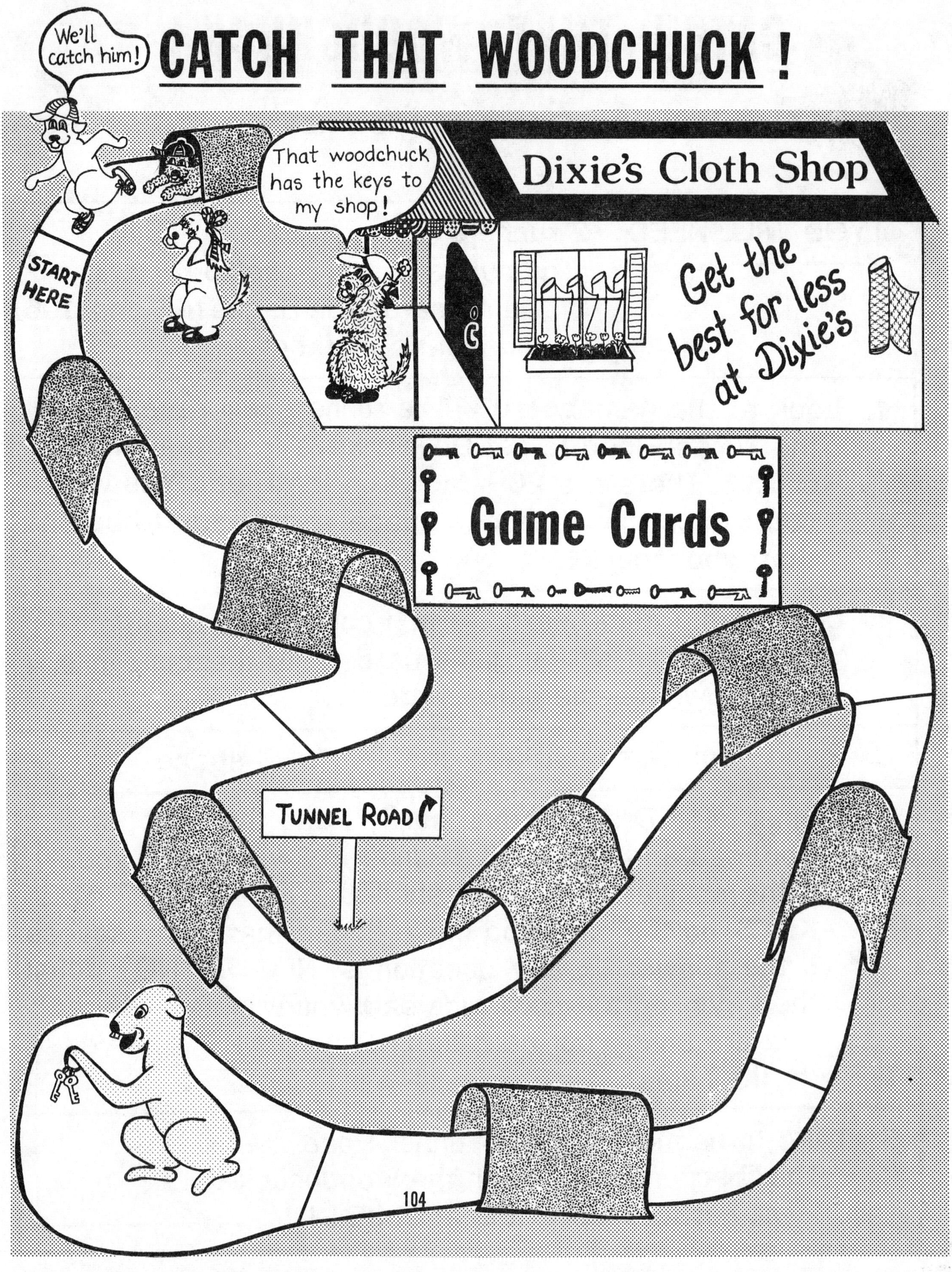

CATCH THAT WOODCHUCK !
(Game ⚷ Cards)

Can a dog shed ? ⚷	Will a ship stop at a dock ? ⚷ ⚷	Can you plan a trip on a ship ? ⚷
Can a class chat ? ⚷	Can a clock tell us when to get up ? ⚷ ⚷	Will a thick dip stick to a chip ? ⚷ ⚷ ⚷
Can a chick peck ? ⚷	Can a whip crack and slap ? ⚷ ⚷	Can you get a cut on your chin ? ⚷
Can a shin grin ? ⚷	Can a glass chip if you drop it ? ⚷ ⚷	Can a clam shut its shell ? ⚷
Can you shop for a chess set ? ⚷ ⚷ ⚷	Can you shut a shed ? ⚷ ⚷	Can you chill a plum ? ⚷
Can a chin sniff ? ⚷	Can you swim to a ship ? ⚷	Can a man sell a shell ? ⚷

105

CATCH THAT WOODCHUCK !
(Game 🔑 Cards)

Can a shed have a lock on it? 🔑	Can the shot of a gun shock you? 🔑🔑
If Sam is thin, then is he slim? 🔑🔑	Can a check chat? 🔑🔑
Can an ax chop a log? 🔑	Can you shuck a cob? 🔑
Can a shack chop a chum? 🔑🔑	Can a ship slip off a cliff? 🔑
Will a hot grill chill a bun? 🔑	Will a vet give a dog a shot? 🔑🔑
Can you put chap stick on your lips? 🔑🔑🔑	Can a whip step on a shed? 🔑🔑

Can a vet give a cat a checkup? 🔑🔑	
Will a dog whiff and sniff? 🔑	
Is your shin on your leg? 🔑	
Do crabs and clams have shells? 🔑🔑🔑	

Final Consonant Blends

2 consonant sounds at the end of a word

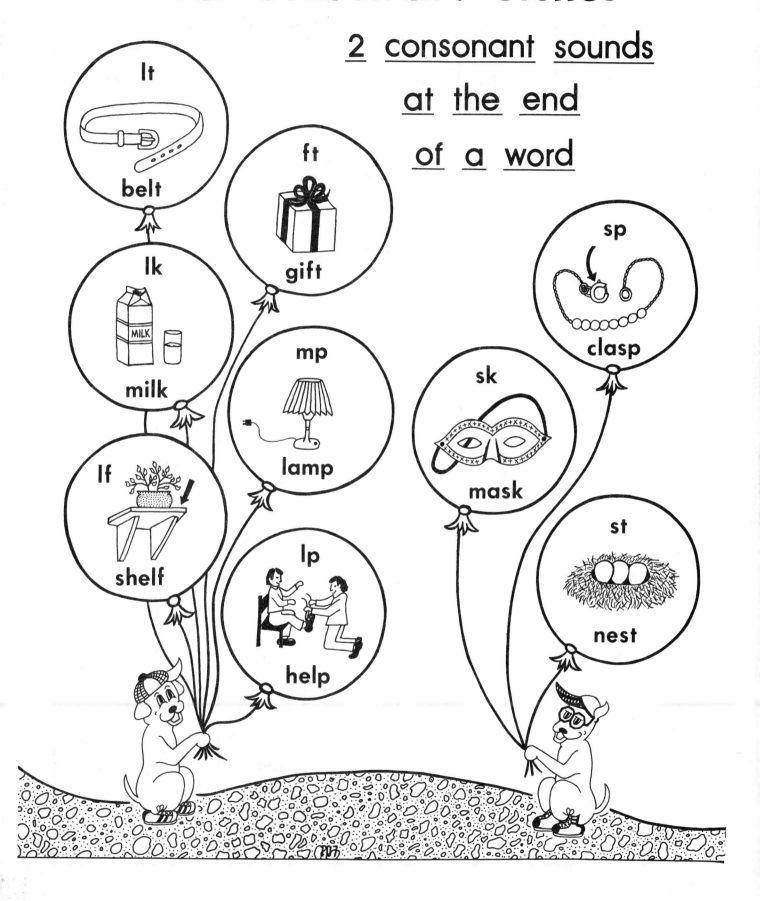

Words to Read and Spell

__ ft

raft	lift
draft	gift
craft	rift
shaft	sift
	drift
heft	swift
left	shift
cleft	
theft	loft
	soft
tuft	

__ lt

belt	hilt
melt	kilt
felt	jilt
welt	quilt
pelt	silt
smelt	tilt
	wilt
cult	stilt
	spilt

__ lp

scalp
help
kelp
yelp
gulp
pulp

__ lk

elk
milk
silk
bulk
hulk
sulk

__ lf

elf
self
shelf
golf
gulf

__ sp

gasp
rasp
clasp
grasp
lisp
crisp

bust
dust
rust
must
gust
just
trust
crust

__ st

cast	best
fast	nest
last	lest
past	pest
mast	jest
blast	quest
	rest
fist	test
list	vest
mist	west
	zest
cost	crest
lost	chest
frost	

__ sk

ask
mask
task
cask
flask
disk
risk
frisk
brisk
whisk
dusk
husk
musk
tusk

__ mp

camp	bump
damp	dump
lamp	hump
ramp	jump
vamp	rump
clamp	lump
stamp	pump
champ	slump
	plump
limp	clump
blimp	trump
primp	grump
crimp	stump
chimp	thump
tromp	romp
stomp	chomp

Sift a Sound with Chef Winston!

NAME_____

DATE_____

On every sifter below, you will see a picture. The **name** of each picture will **end** with _lt, _lk, _lf, or _mp. **Circle** the final consonant blend for every picture.

| lt | lk | lf | | lt | mp | lf | | lf | mp | lk | | lf | lk | lt |

| lf | mp | lk | | lk | mp | lt | | lt | lk | lf | | lt | mp | lk |

| lt | mp | lf | | lk | mp | lt | | lt | lk | lf | | lt | mp | lk |

109

Rhyming Gas Pumps

NAME_____ DATE_____

On every gas pump below, you will see a word ending and a list of letters. Add each of the letters to the word ending and spell rhyming words! Read all your words to your teacher.

Write your words on the numbered blanks!

_ift

g 1_____
l 2_____
dr 3_____

_ump

b 1_____
j 2_____
st 3_____
d 4_____
pl 5_____

_amp

c 1_____
d 2_____
l 3_____
cr 4_____
st 5_____
ch 6_____

_elt

b 1_____
f 2_____
m 3_____

_aft

r 1_____
dr 2_____
cr 3_____

_ilt

t 1_____
w 2_____
qu 3_____

Blast Off with a Consonant Blend!

sk / st / sp

NAME_____

DATE_____

On every rocket below, you will see a picture. The __name__ of each picture will __end__ with _sk, _st, or _sp. __Circle__ the final consonant blend for every picture.

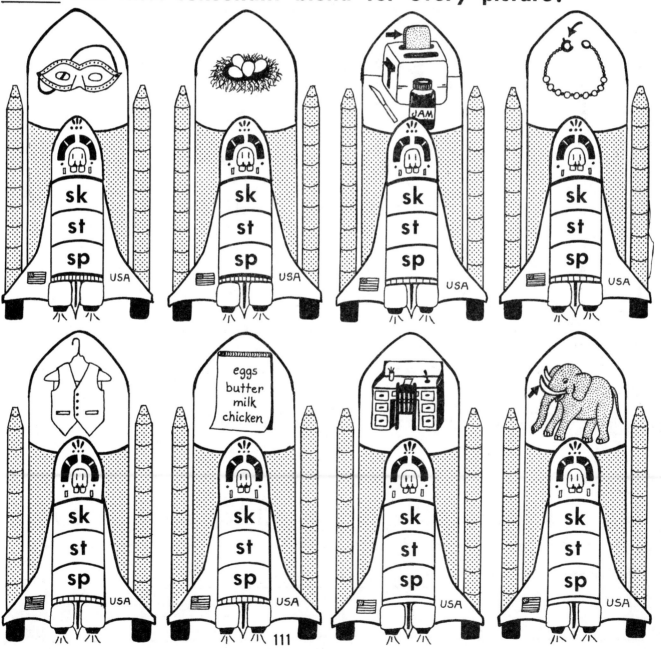

Sign a Cast with Rhyming Words!

NAME_____

DATE_____

On every cast below, you will see a word ending. On every pen, you will see a group of letters. Add each of the letters to the word ending and spell rhyming words! Read all your words to your teacher!

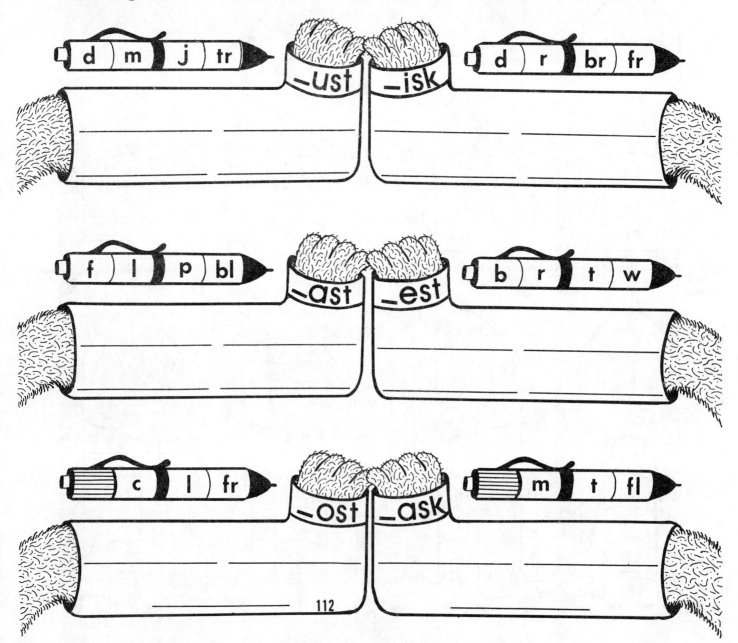

The Camp Street Post Office

NAME

Check ✓ YES or NO.

	YES	NO
Will you see a **lamp** on a **desk**?	○	○
Will you see a **list** of the **costs** of boxes?	○	○
Will you see a **dog** **ask** for **help**?	○	○
Will you see a **dog** sell **stamps**?	○	○

	YES	NO
Will you see a **chimp** with a **gift**?	○	○
Will you see **six eggs** in a **nest**?	○	○
Will you see a **dog** **dust** a **shelf**?	○	○
Will you see a **vest** on a **dog**?	○	○

113

 Color the things you saw!

A Fistful of Missing Vowels

NAME_____ DATE_____

Complete the words on every finger! You must find and fill in the missing vowels. Spell two different words on each fist.

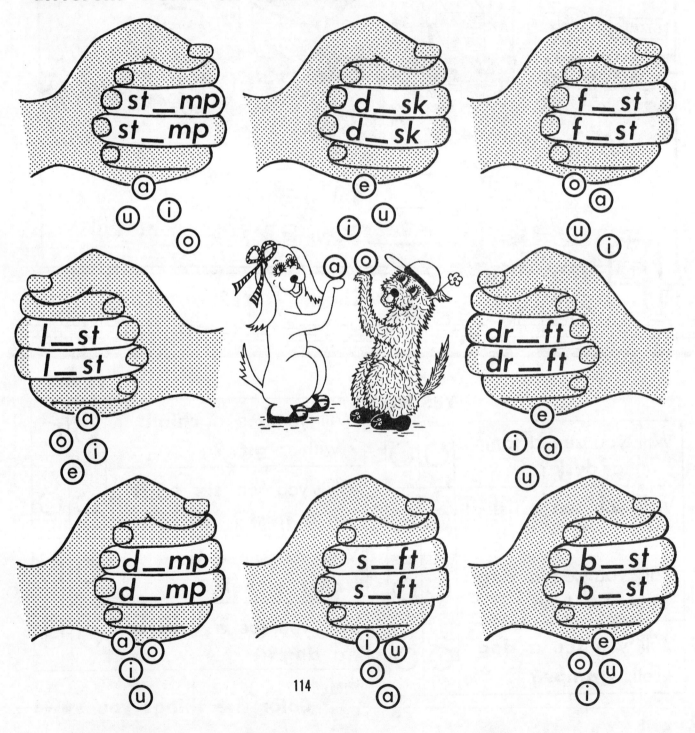

st__mp
st__mp
(a) (i)
(u) (o)

d__sk
d__sk
(e)
(i) (u)
(a) (o)

f__st
f__st
(o) (a)
(u) (i)

l__st
l__st
(a)
(o) (i)
(e)

dr__ft
dr__ft
(e)
(i) (a)
(u)

d__mp
d__mp
(a) (o)
(i)
(u)

s__ft
s__ft
(i) (u)
(o)
(a)

b__st
b__st
(e)
(o) (u)
(i)

114

Dogtown's Raft Race

WELCOME TO THE DOGTOWN POOL!

Pick a racing lane and remember its vowel sound!

YOU WILL NEED : a gameboard (on page 116)

45 word cards (on page 117)

1 announcer

5 raft riders

1. Look at the gameboard.   You will see five swimming lanes on the DOGTOWN POOL. Each raft rider will race down a lane with one of the dogs.

2. Cut out the game cards. Put them in a pile, face down.

3. <u>Announcer</u> : Draw a word card. Read the word to the raft riders. Don't let them see the word!
<u>Raft Riders</u> : Listen to the <u>vowel</u> <u>sound</u> of the word. The racer whose lane has <u>that</u> vowel sound will <u>write</u> <u>the</u> <u>word</u> on the first space of his / her lane.

4. <u>Announcer</u> : Keep drawing and reading word cards, one at a time. Give the raft riders time to write each word.
<u>Raft Riders</u> : Keep splashing down the Dogtown Pool! Write only words that have the vowel sound of <u>your</u> lane.

WHO WINS THE DOGTOWN RAFT RACE ? ? ?
The first raft rider to spell nine words on a lane !

Dogtown's Raft Race

ă   ě   ĭ   ŏ   ŭ

THE WINNER!

116

Dogtown's Raft Race
(word cards)

past	help	lift	dusk	cost
frost	grasp	jump	stomp	stamp
drift	best	mask	risk	desk
must	soft	melt	fist	trust
felt	shift	loft	fast	rust
tromp	bump	chimp	camp	dump
ask	wilt	damp	crust	chest
lisp	test	golf	just	quilt
lost	chomp	left	raft	rest

Final Consonant Blends

2 consonant sounds
at the end
of a word

nt

ant

tent

mint

nd

hand

send

pond

Words to Read and Spell

__ nt		__ nd	
ant	hint	and	end
can't	lint	band	bend
pant	mint	hand	lend
slant	flint	land	mend
plant	print	sand	pend
grant		bland	send
chant	bunt	gland	tend
	hunt	grand	blend
bent	punt	brand	trend
dent	runt	stand	spend
Kent	blunt		
Lent	grunt	bond	wind
rent	stunt	fond	
sent		pond	fund
tent		blond	
vent			
went			
Brent			
spent			

DOGGONE EXCEPTIONS

want
wand
front

Mix a Snack with a Final Blend!

NAME_____ DATE_____

On every blender below, you will see a picture. The **name** of each picture will **end** with _nt or _nd. **Circle** the final consonant blend for every picture.

Send a Plant in a Rhyming Pot!

Read all your words to your teacher!

NAME _____

DATE _____

🐾 On every pot below, you will see a word ending. On the plant leaves, you will see letters. Add each of the letters to the word ending and spell rhyming words! Write your words on the pots.

_and

_int

_end

_unt

_ond

_ent

_ant

121

What's Happening?

NAME_____

DATE_____

 Get ready to match sentences with pictures!

Each sentence below will tell us what is happening in one of the pictures. The sentences are numbered. Put the right sentence number in the corner box of each matching picture.

1. The frog went into the pond!

2. She held the mint in her hand.

3. Mom left the list on the plant stand.

4. Winston will stand in front of the class.

1. J.J. set up a tent!

2. Brent will send the gift to Clint.

3. The plant will bend in the wind.

4. Hal can print his name in the sand.

Final Consonant Blends

nk

2 consonant sounds
at the end
of a word

ng

think

Ping - Pong

Words to Read and Spell

__ nk		
bank	ink	honk
Hank	kink	
yank	link	bunk
sank	mink	dunk
tank	pink	hunk
blank	rink	junk
flank	sink	sunk
plank	wink	flunk
clank	blink	drunk
drank	slink	trunk
frank	clink	plunk
prank	drink	stunk
crank	stink	spunk
stank	think	skunk
spank		chunk
thank		

__ ng	
bang	gong
fang	song
gang	long
rang	tong
hang	prong
sang	thong
tang	strong
slang	
clang	ding
	king
hung	ring
lung	sing
rung	ting
sung	wing
slung	zing
flung	sling
clung	fling
swung	cling
stung	bring
sprung	swing
strung	sting
	thing
	spring
	string

A DOGGONE EXCEPTION

monk

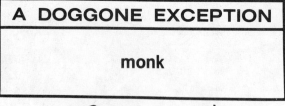

Crank the Tubs with a Consonant Blend!

NAME_____

DATE_____

🐾 Join the dogs for a dish of ice cream! First, you must crank the freezer tubs! Every tub below has a picture on it. The <u>name</u> of each picture will <u>end</u> with _nk or _ng. <u>Circle</u> the final consonant blend for every picture.

Fill a Bank with Rhyming Words!

NAME_____DATE_____

On every piggy bank below, you will see a word ending. On the coins, you will see letters. Add each of the letters to the word ending and spell rhyming words! Write your words on the banks.

Sing-A-Long Dog Songs

NAME_____DATE_____

🐾 Sing a rhyming dog song! On every dog below, you will see a word ending. On the music notes, you will see letters. Add each of the letters to the word ending and spell rhyming words! Write your words on the blanks.

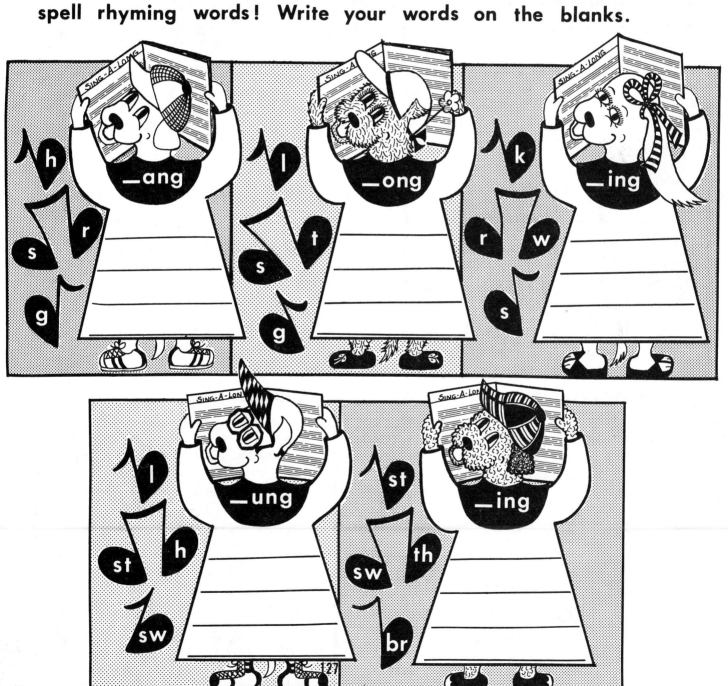

What's Happening?

NAME_____

DATE_____

 Get ready to match sentences with pictures!

Each sentence below will tell us what is happening in one of the pictures. The sentences are numbered. Put the right sentence number in the corner box of each matching picture.

1. The test will ask him to fill in the blanks.

2. She will sing a long song.

3. This skunk will stink if it gets mad!

4. He will thank his dad for the swing set.

1. I think that big bug just stung his trunk!

2. Hank rang the bell for help.

3. Frank will bring a drink to the king.

4. She hung her things on a long rack.

128

Don't Miss That Orangutan Band!

Come see the best band in Dogtown!

YOU WILL NEED: 2 players
a gameboard (on page 130)
36 game cards (on pages 131 and 132)
2 gameboard markers

1. Look at the gameboard. The players will race down the road to get a front row seat at the Orangutan Band concert!

2. Look at the game cards. Each card has a sentence on it. Cut out all the cards. Put them in a pile, face down.

3. Place your markers on the START space.

4. <u>Player #1</u>: Draw a game card. Read the sentence out loud. Player #2 will check you. If you read <u>all</u> the words <u>correctly</u>, COUNT THE MUSIC NOTES on the card and move ahead that many spaces. If you do NOT read all the words correctly, STAY where you are until your next turn. <u>Player #2</u>: Now you do the same.

5. Take turns moving down the road.
   The first player to reach the grandstand...
      will get FREE drinks and snacks at the concert!!

Don't Miss That Orangutan Band!

START HERE

Get that front row seat !

136

Don't Miss That Orangutan Band!
(Game Cards)

A whip will snap when you yank it.	Brent sang a long song.	Mom got a Ping-Pong set from Dad.	I will set the plant on the shelf.	This pen has black ink in it.	A mad bug can sting.
A gun is on the front of a tank.	A test can ask you to fill in a blank.	If the wind is strong, my raft will drift.	I will put a belt on my pants.	I think the pup is a runt.	A gust of wind will bend a stem.
The cast on my hand has a sling.	Clint drank my glass of milk!	A shotgun has a big "BANG!"	My dog has blond spots on his back.	Frank put his glass in the sink.	A skunk will stink if it gets mad!

131

Don't Miss That Orangutan Band!
(Game Cards)

I can hang my cap on the hat rack.	This ox has a brand on his rump!	The bell rang at ten o'clock.	I can pack my tent in the trunk.	A frog will jump into a pond.	I will rest on the bunk bed.
I can put a rock in a slingshot.	Ben will stand up to sing his song.	My dad will spank a bad pet.	I will send a gift to my best pal.	I can mend the rip with a pin.	I must run to the grandstand!
A king will ask for lots of things.	A bug stung him on his chin!	When I box, I swing my fist.	I will print my last name in the sand.	I can swing a golf club.	I will get a mint for a snack.

132

Consonant Digraphs

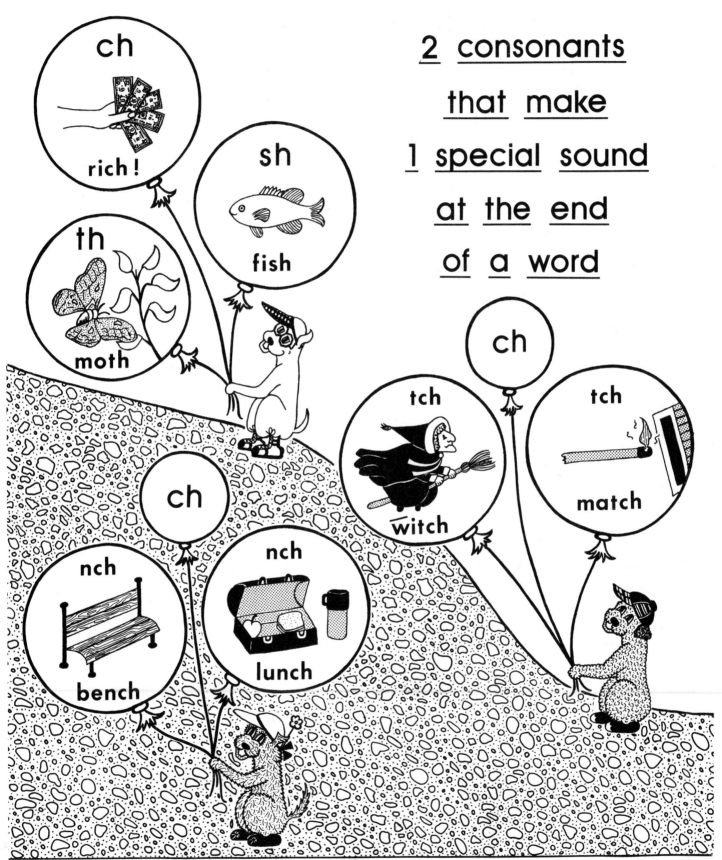

ch — rich!

sh — fish

th — moth

2 consonants that make 1 special sound at the end of a word

ch

tch — witch

tch — match

ch

nch — bench

nch — lunch

Words to Read and Spell

__ sh

ash	gush
bash	hush
cash	lush
dash	mush
gash	rush
mash	blush
hash	slush
lash	flush
rash	plush
sash	crush
slash	brush
flash	shush
clash	
trash	fish
crash	dish
smash	wish
stash	
splash	mesh
	flesh
josh	fresh
slosh	

__ ch

much
such
rich
which

__ nch

ranch	inch
blanch	pinch
branch	clinch
	flinch
bunch	
hunch	bench
lunch	quench
munch	drench
punch	trench
crunch	
brunch	

__ tch

batch	itch
hatch	ditch
latch	hitch
catch	Mitch
match	pitch
patch	witch
snatch	switch
thatch	stitch
scratch	
	etch
	fetch
hutch	sketch
crutch	
clutch	
	blotch
	crotch
	scotch

__ th

bath	moth
math	cloth
path	froth
	broth
pith	
with	Beth
Smith	

DOGGONE EXCEPTIONS

bush	wash	watch
push		swatch

134

Fish for a Consonant Digraph!

NAME_____ DATE_____

On every fish below, you will see a picture. The
<u>name</u> of each picture will <u>end</u> with _sh, _th, or _ch.
<u>Circle</u> the final consonant digraph for every picture.

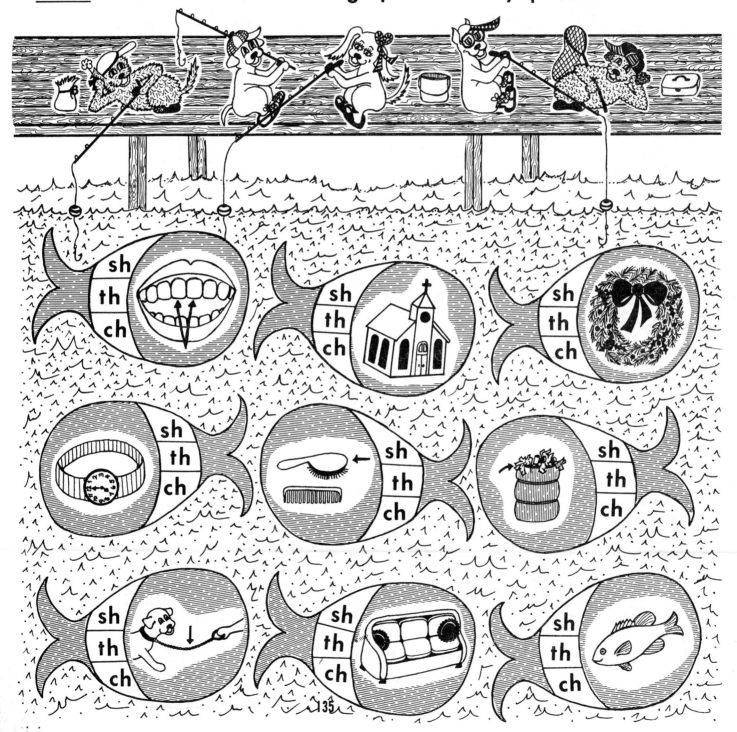

135

Splash Your Words on a Bubble Bath!

NAME_____ DATE_____

🐾 On every bathtub below, you will see a group of letters. On each big bubble, you will see a word ending. Add each of the letters to the word ending and spell rhyming words! Write your words on the blanks.

_ash

| m | d | r | s |

_ish

| f | d | w |

_esh

| fr | | fl |

_ath

| b | m | p |

_ash

| sm | cr | tr | fl |

_ush

| br | h | cr | bl |

Hatch an Egg with a _CH!

NAME _____

The hens need your help to hatch an egg! On every hen, you will see a picture. The __name__ of each picture will __end__ with _tch or _nch. You must __color__ the egg that holds the final consonant sounds for every picture.

137

Rhyming Matches

NAME _____

DATE _____

On every burning match below, you will see a word ending. On the tips of the other matches, you will see letters. Add each of the letters to the word ending and spell rhyming words! Write your words on the matches.

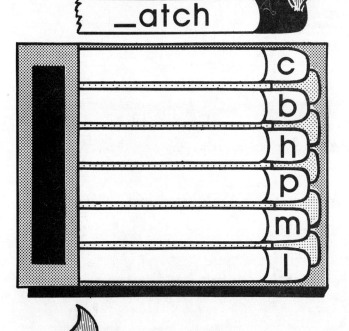

_atch

- c
- b
- h
- p
- m
- l

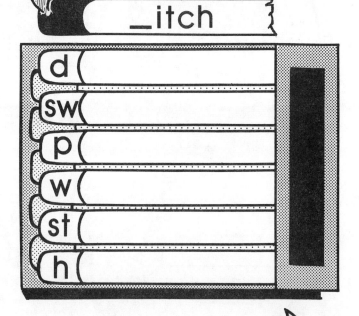

_itch

- d
- sw
- p
- w
- st
- h

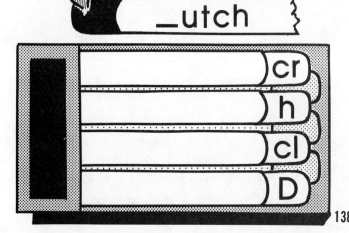

_utch

- cr
- h
- cl
- D

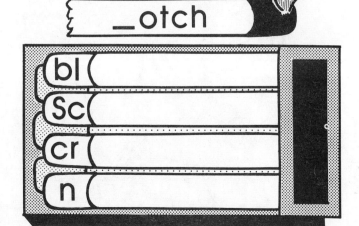

_otch

- bl
- Sc
- cr
- n

Sit on a Rhyming Bench!

NAME_____DATE_____

🐾 On every bench below, you will see a word ending and a group of letters. Add each of the letters to the word ending and spell rhyming words! Write your words on the benches.

p l b cr m br

_unch

Fr dr qu tr b

_ench

139

The Hopscotch Scramble

NAME_____ DATE_____

Join the dogs for 2 games of Hopscotch! On every Hopscotch space, you will see a word ... but the letters are all mixed up! Unscramble the letters and spell words that end with _tch or _nch.

dhitc	atphc		anhrc	ipcnh
_____	_____		_____	_____

ctmah		bnchu
_____		_____

hcfet	chtac		hulnc	chni
_____	_____		_____	_____

wtich
_____

All of the words on this game will **end** with -nch.

pnhcu
_____

ipcth
_____

chneb
_____

All of the words on this game will **end** with -tch.

chruct
crutch

nbrhca
branch

♦ START HERE ♦   ♦ START HERE ♦

140

What's Happening?

NAME_____

DATE_____

 Get ready to match sentences with pictures!

Each sentence below will tell us what is happening in one of the pictures. The sentences are numbered. Put the right sentence number in the corner box of each matching picture.

1. This cat will get fresh fish in his dish!

2. Which dog will get the wish?

3. Mitch will catch the moth with his net.

4. The dog will rush to fetch the stick.

1. If you flip the switch, the lamp will flash on.

2. This man must be rich. He has so much cash!

3. The witch had a cup of punch for lunch.

4. Beth will dust the bench with a soft cloth.

THE DOGTOWN LOTTERY

Pick the best tickets and WIN the cash!

YOU WILL NEED: 2 players
a gameboard (on page 143)
30 game cards (on pages 144, 145 and 146)
2 pennies (for game markers)
2 pencils
2 sheets of writing paper

1. Look at the gameboard. The lottery players will move down the path of coins to win the chest that holds the Dogtown cash!

2. Look at the game cards. These will be your lottery tickets. Each card has a riddle and three answers on it. Cut out all the cards. Put them in a pile, face down, on the game-board.

3. Place your pennies on the START space, just behind the first coin.

4. Player #1: Draw a lottery ticket. Read the riddle and all three answers out loud. Pick the answer that you think is right and write it on your sheet of paper. Player #2 will check you. If your answer is correct, COUNT THE DOTS on your ticket and jump ahead that many coins. If your answer is NOT correct, STAY where you are until your next turn. Player #2: Now you do the same.

5. Keep drawing, reading, and answering riddles, one at a time. The first player to reach the chest of cash... will WIN the DOGTOWN LOTTERY!!

THE DOGTOWN LOTTERY

Pick the best tickets and WIN the cash!

START HERE

LOTTERY TICKETS

CASH

CASH

143

THE DOGTOWN LOTTERY
Game Cards

You can dust a desk with it.
It will rub on a thick wax.

You sing it.
It can be glad or sad.
It can be long.

a cat
a chick
a chin

a rat
a dog
a plum

a shelf
a cloth
a rug

a song
a doll
a frog

She can peck!
Her mom is a hen.
an egg.
She will hatch from

It will shed.
It can fetch a stick.
It can sniff and lick.

You can catch it in a net.
It can be a pest.
It can sting!

a quilt
the sun
a fan

It can be just a scratch or a big gash.
It can sting and swell!

a duck
a bug
a pig

It can stop a chill.
It is soft.
your lap.
You can toss it on

a pal
a witch
a mom

a cut
a cast
a crash

a pet
a class
a clock

You grip it with your hand.
You can spell with it.
It has ink in it.

She can cast a spell!
black hat.
This gal has on a big

will ring.
It has a bell that
You can plug it in.
It can tick.

a bat
a pen
a lid

THE DOGTOWN LOTTERY
Game Cards

You can catch it in a pond.

It can swim fast.

It can be your lunch!

He will swing from branch to branch.

He will munch on a bunch of bananas!

---

the sand

the wind

the mud

---

lunch
dip
milk

a hog
a ram
a fish

---

a dad
a chimp
a moth

A swift gust will send a draft in.

When it is strong, the dust is bad.

You can drink it from a glass.

You can spill it.

You can chill it.

You can splash in it.
You can fill it with suds.

It is next to the sink.

---

a belt
a lamp
a whip

It can pinch.

It can run in the sand.

It has a shell.

---

a bathtub

a pond

a glass

It has a plug on it.

If you flip the switch, it will blink on and off.

---

a ship
a cab
a bus

a crab
a hand
a clamp

---

an ant

an ox

an ax

It can trick a rat with a quick snap!

It has a deck on it.
It must stop at a dock to get gas.

You will see him help a man with a crop.

He is big and strong.

---

a track

a bump

a trap

145

THE DOGTOWN LOTTERY
Game Cards [LOTTERY TICKET]

You will print your name on it.
It will ask you to add.
You can check it.

You drag it up a hill.
You sit on it.
It will drop fast on a slick path!

• a plant
grass
a bench

•• a bunk
a bank
a blank

a plus
a math test
a list ••

a sled
a sock
a trunk ••

You can sit and rest on it.
You can clip, trim, or cut it.

It has a slot on the top of it. You fill it up with a lot of cash!

You grasp them with your hands.
You will swing them.
You put them in a bag.

• a pin
a clip
a patch

A hen will sit in it.

An egg will hatch in it.

chips
pans
golf clubs ••

You must stitch it on.
This will mend a rip in your pants.

• a bed
a shed
a shack

a truck
a nest
a swing •

• a dress
a list
a bag

It has a big "BANG!"

Dad can hunt elk with it.

You can rest or nap on it. A mom will tuck you into it.

Mom must have it to shop. She can print it on a pad.

a tan bag
a shotgun
a big tent ••